EXMOOR INTERLUDE

EXMOOR INTERLUDE

Mary Rose Baker

ATHENA PRESS
LONDON

First Published 2005 by
ATHENA PRESS
Queen's House, 2 Holly Road
Twickenham TW1 4EG
United Kingdom

Printed for Athena Press

*For my husband John
and grandson Michael,
with love*

Preface

This book is the sequel to *Memoirs of our Farming Days*, which ended with our move to Exmoor. My final sentence, 'But that is another story…' has led to many people asking when the story will be ready, so here it finally is. *Memoirs* told of our daring decision to exchange a cosy urban-type existence in Somerset for a far from comfortable life on a small farm in North Devon. There followed fifteen exciting years of anxious, and sometimes hilarious, times. Overall it was a most satisfying life.

John's Uncle Ken watched our progress with keen interest. He was a retired farmer living at South Hill Farm, Withypool, in the heart of Exmoor. A few years previously he had encouraged us to keep a caravan on his camping field, to use for weekends and holidays, and we enjoyed great times there. When Uncle discovered we were looking for a small farm for ourselves he tried to persuade us to have a permanent caravan sited near his house and suggested several ways we could make a living there. It was a tempting offer, especially as we were very fond of him and of Aunt Dolly. However, we already had plans for a small dairy herd, in which he had little interest or knowledge.

We finally found a farmhouse with dairy, outbuildings and fourteen acres in Chittlehamholt, North Devon. Later we rented a further sixteen acres, which enabled us to live there comfortably and quite cheaply.

After fourteen years it seemed that we would be very happy to remain at Kinnings, possibly for the rest of our lives. It was not to be! One evening towards the end of

1985 we visited Uncle Ken and received some startling news. He informed John that he was leaving South Hill to him in his will. Aunt Dolly had died about two years previously. They had no children and although John was his next of kin, being his brother's eldest son, this news was completely unexpected. We were speechless! He then told us he was lonely and that South Hill needed a man there to keep it together, so would we consider moving in with him? There was no way we could give an immediate answer and he understood this, as he knew how happy we were on our own little farm. He assured us it would make no difference to his will. Should we decide to stay at Kinnings we could always sell South Hill when he died.

Two days passed before we could agree on a decision. Although we loved South Hill we didn't really want to move. Yet how could we disappoint Uncle when he was being so kind to us? So I wrote, thanking him, and saying we would be very happy to come with him and we would put our farm on the market in the spring. It sold the same day that the notice was put up at our top gate, and in June 1986 we arrived at South Hill.

Chapter One

I awoke that fine June morning to the strident crowing of a cockerel beneath my window; a joyous sound that I had been missing for the past few years. I realised it was Uncle Ken's favourite bird greeting us on our first day in South Hill, this beautiful farm on Exmoor, once described to us by an estate agent as the 'jewel in the crown'. Looking through the window I could see the tents and caravans scattered around the camping field below. All was quiet so far but I spotted one man walking alongside the river with his dog. The cockerel crowed again and birds were singing in nearby trees. It seemed, this morning, that all was right with the world. I climbed back into bed.

John was still sleeping soundly. I knew that we were both going to miss Kinnings, the little farm where we had enjoyed living and working for fifteen years. But South Hill had always been our first love, ever since the time when we had been persuaded to keep our caravan in the field. In those days we had spent every weekend and all our annual holidays here, loving every minute of it. We would often stand beside the caravan, gazing up at the 'big house' and wondering what it would feel like to live there. Not that the farmhouse was very big, but its location was perfect. It seemed an impossible dream at that time but dreams can come true, for here we were now sharing Uncle Ken's home. Since losing his wife, Dolly, he had suffered increasingly poor health and was badly in need of company and help.

It was fun having breakfast together for the first time, especially with Uncle being so cheerful and showing how delighted he was to have us with him. Mike, our grandson, had just left school for the last time and had turned up to provide extra assistance. After breakfast Uncle opened his front door, put a chair there and sat in the sun for a considerable time, while we three set to work. I was busy in the kitchen, checking the foodstuffs for 'best before' dates, tidying cupboards and so on while the men busied themselves with jobs outside.

Our generator arrived from Kinnings and was established in an outhouse. At least any power cuts would not affect us now. Next we arranged for an electrician to rewire the house and buildings. We needed this urgently as it was still on round pin sockets which were unsuitable for our freezer, microwave and electric iron – all items which Uncle didn't possess. Aunt Dolly had always heated black irons on the Rayburn. Fortunately the electrician came the very next day although it was a Sunday!

Uncle was very taken up with Mike. 'Can you drive a car boy?' he asked him.

'Not yet,' Mike replied, 'I'm only sixteen.'

'Time you learnt to drive in a field then.'

Off they went in the Subaru down to a level field near the river. They returned much later, instructor and learner both well pleased with themselves. By the time he returned home a few days later he was quite a proficient driver, having been allowed to take the car on his own, even up and down the lane, and he was so grateful to his great, great uncle for the opportunity. He had previously driven our tractor at Kinnings, but this was different.

Our dog, Bess, was so excitable over the move and with so much happening here that we had to fix her up with comfortable quarters in one of the barns. Bringing her into the kitchen was a disaster. She chased around like a lunatic, never still for a moment until Uncle remarked dryly, 'If thic was my dog I'd shoot her!' He was only joking of course, as he was very fond of dogs.

We took her out for regular walks in the top fields and Uncle came with us one day. He pointed out the damage the badgers had done digging enormous setts under some of the hedges, also the weeds in the fields and the general signs of neglect. He was also upset that his open-sided hay barn in the lane was leaning over, the poles holding it up having given way.

'If that was put right I'd start to feel better,' he said.

We managed to get Raymond Jenkins and his son Paul to come and help set it upright, which pleased Uncle greatly. Raymond had kept a caravan in Uncle's field years ago, the same time as we did. He and Sylvia, whose home was in Bristol, fell in love with Withypool and bought a small farm here while we were at Kinnings. It was only a short distance along the road from South Hill and we were pleased to have friends as neighbours.

John had started to decorate the small spare room which led off the main bedroom. Cathy, our grand-daughter, was bringing a friend to stay in about three weeks' time and this room would do nicely for them.

While John was busy decorating, Uncle suggested we drove along the road in the direction of Hawkridge, as there was something he was anxious to see. To my surprise he suddenly turned off the road onto a grassy section of the moor. Soon we were driving through great ruts in the ground, so deep in places that the car was thrown almost on to its side. I was frightened that we were in danger of turning over. I glanced at Uncle and was surprised to see tears running down his cheeks.

'I was told about this,' he sobbed. 'I had to see it for myself. I know who did it.'

The way ahead looked even worse.

'Let's try and get back on the road,' I pleaded nervously.

After much scary manoeuvring we finally made it and soon reached home safely, and in silence. This episode was never mentioned again but I have often wondered about it since.

That evening, when the three of us relaxed in the cosy warm kitchen, Uncle said he wanted a serious talk with us. He was suggesting some codicils to his will. First of all he decided he wanted us to have the seventy acres at South Batsom as he thought the forty at South Hill wouldn't be sufficient for us to make a comfortable living. We were very surprised but said immediately that we didn't need this, especially as it might cause trouble with the person who was expecting to be left it. In retrospect we had cause to regret this hasty decision. The second thing he wanted was to make sure his fishing rights at Batsom remained with South Hill in order that it could continue to be used by campers and fishermen, as at present. The third thing was to leave his car, the Subaru, to John.

These two wishes we agreed to and he decided to write to his solicitor straight away. He was eighty-seven years old and he appeared to have a premonition that he would not live much longer. We did not see what he wrote but we posted the letter for him the following day. Fortunately the furniture was all ours. This was an agreement he made when he wanted us to sell all of ours before we moved and he said everything at South Hill would then belong to us.

We were very anxious about Uncle's health. His appetite was very poor although we were trying all his favourite meals and getting him whatever he fancied. He said he would soon be better and that the doctor had been pleased with him when he saw him recently.

Another upset was the realisation that Charlie cockerel was missing. The following day a white hen went missing, and then yet another one disappeared. Obviously a fox was around; we had found a pile of feathers nearby. At one time Uncle would have kept guard and shot the fox but he was unable to do that now, and we didn't feel like it.

It was a very busy time for us. The camping field was full of tents and caravans, with campers regularly knocking at the kitchen door on arrival or departure. Many of them came regularly every year so wanted to chat with 'Kenny Baker'. We had to be introduced to them and found them very pleasant people on the whole.

There were chicks hatching out in the barn and a second hen sitting on eggs in a pigsty. Also we had fetched seven Muscovy ducks from Kings Nympton. Uncle loved having the birds running around but we insisted they were now shut in at night because of the fox, which we hoped would keep away in the daytime with so many people around.

John soon finished decorating the spare room and as soon as we had put in two single beds, a small wardrobe and a chair it was ready for Uncle's inspection. He was really delighted. In fact, he was absolutely amazed at how large it appeared now.

'I'm looking forward to the girls coming soon,' he said. 'I do like young people about.'

South Hill was very well arranged upstairs. The staircase was in the centre of the house. The landing had a short passage on the right leading to the bathroom and two bedrooms, and the same with two bedrooms on the left. Uncle had recently had a toilet and washbasin fitted in his room, so the girls would not interfere with him but would be in the room leading from ours. We planned more alterations later, but not until Uncle's health improved.

Chapter Two

On 23 July 1986 the wedding of Prince Andrew and Sarah Ferguson took place. Uncle was looking forward to watching this on television and settled himself in his comfortable chair in readiness.

The previous evening he had complained of severe pains, went to bed early but didn't want the doctor. Today he was no better and we knew that we must send for his doctor, who fortunately arrived in a very short time.

After a private examination he came out to us, looking very anxious.

'I'm afraid he has a blockage and will need to go into hospital straight away.'

He phoned for an ambulance while we put together the few things Uncle needed to take. The hospital was in Taunton, about twenty-five miles away, which made it difficult for visiting, but we promised to go the following evening.

He was very bright when we saw him and in less pain. It was arranged that we would visit every other evening and other people went on alternate nights. The next visit was more promising. He waved as soon as he saw us entering the ward and said he felt much better and fancied meals again.

John started work on the second small bedroom, next to Uncle's. The whole house had become rather shabby and badly needed some paint and wallpaper to cheer it up.

We looked forward to our next visit to tell Uncle about the decorating, about the new chicks that were hatching and about the influx of campers. Many of them were regulars who had sent messages to him, hoping to see him home again before they left. Unfortunately, after eating he was now in pain again and very unhappy. We realised he would not be home just yet so decided we had time to paint his bedroom. We knew he would appreciate it looking fresh and bright on his return home.

Our next visit found him back on a drip, but he seemed happier and so keen to hear all the farm news. He wanted to know if a letter had come from his solicitor. This actually arrived two days later, together with his amended will. He opened it, read it and then passed it to John.

'See if it's all there,' he said anxiously. 'Is it what I wanted?'

He was looking so ill that we couldn't tell him that it wasn't really clear about the fishing rights. This could be put right when he was better. Apart from this it was all in order so we let him sign it. The man in the next bed had two visitors and they were willing to witness his signature, leaving Uncle very relieved.

Before he went into hospital we had been enjoying a spell of dry, sunny weather. Now it had become unsettled with rain, often wet all day. It seemed in keeping with this unhappy period. There were even more campers arriving, as expected, at the end of July, and it was depressing to see them wading around in wellies and raincoats. At least they had come prepared and no one was grumbling. They were only worried about Kenny Baker.

We wished the hospital had been nearer, as we found fifty miles driving after a busy day was very tiring, especially the night when we returned home to find the pump had packed up and it took until midnight fixing a new one!

Next, we heard that Uncle was to have an operation. No visitors were allowed that day but the following evening we went, hoping for good news. Unfortunately we found him in a very poor state. He had difficulty in speaking to us, was very depressed and looked terrible. The operation had revealed bowel cancer so we realised it would take time for him to recover.

Earlier that day John had collected Cathy and Denise from South Molton and they were quite happy to stay alone in the evening answering the phone for bookings, or enquiries about Uncle's health.

We were quite late getting to bed that night and were soon asleep. At 1 a.m. we were awakened by the insistent ringing of the telephone. It was the hospital, informing us that Uncle had passed away. I suppose we should have expected this but we didn't. It was a dreadful shock as we were very fond of him and would certainly feel lost on our own without him. We had been at South Hill for just six weeks.

The girls were upset by the news but we found time to take them to Minehead in the evening. There was so much to attend to. We arranged the funeral with our vicar, John Atkin – cremation in Taunton Deane crematorium on Thursday 14th August. The vicar was wonderfully helpful and sympathetic, as he also had lost a good friend.

During a long conversation with us he spoke of one problem he had to solve. It concerned a cat whose elderly owner had gone into hospital and he had been asked to find it a kind home, so far with no success. I knew he was hoping we might volunteer and of course we did! We loved cats and knew we needed one or more mice catchers on the farm. Our family turned up on Sunday but Iain and Mike (who had just started his first job) had to go home ready for work on Monday. They took Denise back with them. Cathy and Maggie stayed with us to help out until after the funeral.

Chicks were still hatching out; John fetched a trailer load of our hay from Chittlehamholt; we went to Minehead to collect Uncle's will from his solicitor and we cleaned and tidied up at the house.

The weather had been very unsettled for some days but we were fortunate to have a fine day for the funeral, which made a sad occasion a little more bearable. There was a good attendance.

Cathy had stayed at home preparing a very tempting buffet, and several campers joined in to enjoy this. Unfortunately, Raymond and Sylvia mistook the time of the funeral, arrived at the crematorium when it was all over and so missed the meal! Maggie and Cathy later returned home.

The following evening, Pippa was brought to us by a farmer's wife who had been caring for her temporarily and was glad to pass her on. She was a poor little creature, very thin and rather elderly. She was extremely nervous and had been scared of the dogs on the farm. I felt sure that Bess would not worry her as she had ignored our two cats at Kinnings. We put down a little food and water but, as we expected, she didn't want food yet. She was better pleased, though, with a cardboard box in front of the Rayburn.

It was a fine, sunny day for the Withypool flower show, but we were too busy to go this year. We had some army cadets arrive with their captain and needed to show them where to camp this time. They came each year but we had not met them before. It was fascinating to watch them gather outside the farmhouse each evening for their ceremony, a bugle sounding the retreat and the flag lowered. In the morning it was the reveille – to wake up.

Next day our friend Beryl Waldron came for the day. It was her first visit to South Hill. Such a pity it was raining and not looking so good outside but there would be more visits for that. In the meantime we had plenty to chat about. It was so good to have visitors and to have the campers around. Otherwise John and I would have felt very lonely without Uncle Ken.

Maggie and family arrived for the August bank holiday weekend. Mike was pleased with his eight 'O' levels and Maggie with her one for Psychology and Child Development. They set to work straight away, Iain putting up a shelf in the larder and Mike cleaning the duck house and pond and cutting the grass outside the house.

Bank holiday Monday was a terrible day, with torrential rain and gales which caused the river to rise and the camping field to become really soggy. Our family had arranged to return home anyway but two lots of campers left because of the weather. Two days later another family only managed to get as far as the village shop. They abandoned their caravan and returned to ask if John could tow it up the hill out of Withypool. Their daughter was sick over our dining table before they finally left! Later, John had to tow a car out of the ditch into which it had slipped from the lane.

During a short spell of improved weather we drove to Taunton to collect Uncle's ashes, then on to Barnstaple to buy a larger dining table and chairs. This replaced the present rickety one which had almost collapsed when we were all sitting round it at the weekend. John had been busy painting some bedroom furniture and now started on the outside walls of the house.

The water tank, housed in a lean-to attached to the barn and facing the house, was leaking badly. The water supply here was a complicated affair. It came from a good spring in a field, ran by gravity to this tank and was then pumped to a holding tank in the lane above the house and finally ran to the house by gravity. There was usually a reasonable supply but with dozens of campers filling their containers, pulling the flush etc., it needed only a long spell of dry weather to set us worrying. We were fortunate to see a fibreglass tank advertised which we bought to replace the leaking one, and this proved to be very satisfactory.

Chapter Three

We had several fine days in September so John was able to get on with painting outside. The camping field was quieter now, as children had returned to school.

Myra, an old school friend, came to stay for a few days and it was lovely to show off South Hill to her. She was fascinated by everything she saw around Withypool.

'When I told people I was coming here,' she remarked, 'they had never heard of it. In fact they didn't know Exmoor at all.'

'Just as well,' I replied. 'It's special because it's so quiet. There is no public transport so we can only get hikers from time to time. Cars often pass straight through the village on their way to better known locations.'

We decided to go for a walk. We crossed over the stepping stones at the end of our lane and walked along the other bank of the River Barle towards Tarr Steps, although we didn't go all the way there on that occasion. Tarr Steps is an ancient clapper bridge and is a very popular beauty spot in the Exmoor National Park. Coming back along the river we saw many dragonflies and heard the occasional splash of a brown trout. I was sorry that Myra was too early to see the salmon leaping on their way to spawn.

Our family came again for the weekend; they usually brought rain with them and sure enough we had the first rain for several days! It was cold as well. John had arranged to fetch another load of hay from Sam's and set off early before the rain started. Mr Wright, Sam's father, gave John a large box of vegetables from his garden. Very acceptable, as we had none of our own yet. Mike cleaned out buildings ready for calves which we hoped to buy soon.

On Sunday morning, Maggie and Cathy came to church with us to an early morning service, including Holy Communion, taken by John Atkin. We always enjoyed a friendly greeting from him. St Andrews is a fairly small church but considering the population of Withypool the congregation is quite good. After this, the vicar had to hurry off to take a service in the next village. He had to fit in four churches in all but not all of them in one day.

Although still cold, it was dry again, so we took Myra to Dulverton in the afternoon. It is a beautiful drive to Dulverton across the moors. The sheep graze there unfenced, so they frequently cross, or lie in, the road, unperturbed by the traffic. This is their land – motorists are the trespassers! There were also a few ponies and cattle wandering there.

Dulverton is a small pretty town with narrow streets, shops, a fine church and a medieval bridge over the River Barle. Myra really enjoyed this outing before returning to her own home again. Meanwhile the family wandered around South Hill and then left for home after tea. Myra is Maggie's godmother but they live some distance from each other, so it was good for them to meet up here.

Pippa was less nervous now and eating well. Cathy had made a fuss of her at the weekend, deciding to take her for a walk with a string lead. After a few yards she easily slipped out of it and scurried away. We couldn't find her and it was some time before she finally returned. Later, Cathy nursed her and we were horrified to see a number of large fleas crawling on her pretty pink jumper!

Next morning, we heard a scratching noise on our bedroom door and were amazed to discover Pippa outside. How she had managed to open the heavy, latched kitchen door we never discovered but it happened again, so we managed to secure it with baler cord. Her next trick was to open a cupboard door under the sink and hide, unseen, behind the saucepans. With her light grey fur and being so small, and keeping so quiet, it was difficult to locate her at first. Each night, every door had to be secured with baler cord, quite a performance. At least the fleas had been successfully removed.

We decided to get a second cat! I definitely wanted a black and white one this time so when I saw one advertised in our local paper I immediately telephoned. I was disappointed to hear that a blue Burmese must come with him – I didn't want this. All other callers had only wanted the Burmese. Their owner had just died and it was her last wish that her two cats should not be separated. Fortunately, I was told there would be another black and white available in a couple of days. He had just been rescued and needed to be castrated before being homed. Mary Redfern, who lived in Minehead, was attached to an animal charity so needed to inspect our home first and then deliver him to us.

He arrived three days later – a large, beautifully marked cat who I immediately fell in love with, named Thomas. I thought Mary looked rather anxious as she released him from the carrier.

'He's been having a bad time of it in Minehead,' she explained. 'His owners moved house and left this young cat behind. It appears that he has been fending for himself for almost two years, sneaking into houses for food and terrorising the ladies of Minehead when they tried to shoo him out! It has left him rather wild.'

I sat on a chair and spoke to him and, to Mary's surprise, he jumped onto my lap and started purring. He realised he had found a home at last. Then he bit me!

Life with Thomas was always surprising, usually he was very affectionate, then, without warning, would come the nip. On one occasion he scratched me, leaving little beads of blood spurting across the back of my hand. Once when John was stroking him Thomas bit his nose, leaving him somewhat disfigured for a week or two! We always forgave him and blamed it on the ill treatment he had suffered in his short life. At least he never attacked little Pippa, although she hissed at him whenever they met.

John was busy painting the back of the house during another spell of fine weather. The inside could be dealt with during the winter.

It was quieter in the camping field now, just a couple of caravans turning up. Also a group of junior leaders who were able to camp in the field this time. When it was wet they had the use of an outbuilding. After they left we were annoyed to find that they had pinched some best timber we had bought recently and used it on their fires.

We saw in the local newspaper that the black and white and Burmese cats were still wanting homes together. There was a lovely photograph of them. We rang Mary Redfern two days later to see if anyone had offered yet. They hadn't so, to her delight, we said we would take them. She brought them straight away: Jack, with markings almost identical to Thomas and Christopher, the pedigree Burmese. They settled in well and soon all four were lying together in front of the

Rayburn, with Jack and Christopher interlocked with each other.

The first Sunday evening in October we had the harvest service in church, followed by supper in the village hall. There was a splendid buffet set out on tables through the centre of the hall, with seats around the outside. There were sandwiches, various savouries and dishes of trifles and fruit salad. All quite delicious. We did not know many of the village folk at this time, but John Atkin was there to chat to us. He had already seen us at the farm since Uncle's funeral. He had recently visited Pippa's owner, Mrs Sally Page-Williams, in Minehead hospital and told her that Pippa was happy with us.

'If you are in Minehead any time do visit her,' he suggested. 'She would love to meet you.'

The family had a short visit to us at the weekend, arriving mid-afternoon on Saturday, as Cathy had been playing her clarinet in an orchestra that morning. They had to leave us on Sunday afternoon for Cathy to have confirmation instruction in the evening.

The next day we visited Sally in hospital and showed her photographs of Pippa, taken in our kitchen. She was quite excited when we gave them to her but was rather tearful about her 'Pippa-puss'. She knew she would never be able to look after her again as she had already given up her home.

The first hunt since we moved here had just taken place. I was amazed to see several cars driving past our house and realised they were hunt followers. I rushed out in a furious temper, shouting at the first driver that they were not allowed here. Although we unfortunately have a right of way for walkers and horses there is a notice on our top gate that vehicles should be for South Hill Farm only. These people had obviously heard that we were new at the farm so had decided to try it on. The man I shouted at looked rather shamefaced and apologised profusely. I don't know how they managed to back out, up a very long, rough and twisting lane, but they never came again!

No one connected with hunting was welcome, but we had to endure the horse-riders, with their dogs chasing around as if they owned the place.

They killed a stag that day and next day we had a joint of venison brought to us. We certainly didn't fancy eating an animal which had been chased for miles, but our four cats were very appreciative!

It was time to start farming again. We had been watching calf prices and decided they were too expensive, but there was little sign of them falling so we went to Barnstaple with the intention of buying. We wanted young Hereford x Friesian bull calves which we would rear for about five months and then sell on as stirks. We had been very successful with these at Kinnings and it was something we enjoyed doing.

Our favourite dealer, John May, had previously bought many calves on our behalf so we approached him again. He always knew if a calf was likely to do well. Also if the price would allow us to make a profit. The trouble was that market prices were so unpredictable. They might well have fallen in five months' time, but we had to take a chance.

It was so interesting to watch the calves being sold, but on this occasion there was only one suitable for us: a lively little bull calf who drank well. It was seven days before he had the company of three other similar calves, all of these purchased in the Friday Barnstaple market. They averaged about £120 each. A week later we had two further bulls and this time one of them refused to drink. Also the prices had risen.

We now decided to buy heifer calves, and five of these averaged only £42 each. These eleven would keep us satisfied for a while. Unfortunately one of the heifers also refused milk but drank a glucose drink with relish. The bull would still drink only plain water and caused us a little anxiety for a while, but eventually he started to run around like the others. He had probably been with his mother for some time before coming to market. We missed having our own cows because reluctant calves would always drink from a cow.

Anyway, they all did well for us at four to five months, with the heifers fetching £140 each and the bulls £235 and £240.

We heard that Michael had been in Frenchay Hospital having four wisdom teeth removed. It left him in considerable pain and unable to eat for a while, but once the stitches were out he felt much better.

We loved walking around our fields. Bess was always waiting to come but we were so amused when three of the cats started to join us. Pippa, the old lady, stayed quietly at home. Christopher liked to climb a tree now and again, but Thomas and Jack walked very sedately. This walk became a regular occurrence on fine days, but there was a snag. So far we have been walking to church on Sunday mornings – up our long, steep lane and down the road to the village. Now Thomas wanted to come there with us! Our only way to avoid him was to go by car. The first time we did this we found, on our return, that Thomas was waiting just inside our top gate. We couldn't leave him near the road, neither would he come inside the car. John tried to grab him in the hedge, and when his glasses fell off he stepped on them and shattered them! Luckily, Thomas had enough of this and didn't follow the car in future.

Now, at the end of October, we had started decorating indoors. First, painting and papering the hall and stairs. It was a wide, impressive staircase – varnished wood, with just a thin rope to hold on to, which I found difficult with an arthritic knee. Once it was carpeted and a handrail fitted it was much easier and looked really good.

Next we tackled the small living room, which was overcrowded with furniture. Uncle had suggested that if I didn't need the piano, Cathy might like it, but she preferred to keep her own, so we sold ours. Raymond removed a stove which jutted out in front of the fireplace and took up a considerable space. The odd chairs went to the salerooms with many other items. Now we could paint, paper, re-carpet and hang new curtains. A three-piece suite and a nest of tables fitted easily into the empty room, which now seemed much larger and suitable for entertaining friends.

We were getting invitations. We spent a day with Beryl Waldron in Chittlehampton and, later on, a day with Myra in Somerton. It was unusual to have so much leisure time. I actually started a jigsaw puzzle.

David Harris, a former neighbour, called in on his way back from Cutcombe livestock market, giving us all the latest gossip from Chittlehamholt.

Our favourite markets were South Molton on Thursdays and Barnstaple on Fridays. We usually went to these every week because we met so many of our friends. Also we liked to watch the animals, even when we weren't buying or selling.

We enjoyed the shops in Barnstaple. We had only one small shop with post office in Withypool, providing milk and groceries. There were petrol pumps and toilets across the road. Apart from the church, a pub and village hall, a small number of houses and the outlying farms, there were just the moors beyond, which made it so special. In late summer we enjoyed mile upon mile of purple heather and ling, interspersed with golden gorse, glistening in the sun. The little river trickling through completed the picture.

Our calves were now doing well and growing. John dehorned them all and castrated the bulls. He went along the road to help Raymond with his two calves which wouldn't drink.

We killed off four bantams which were not laying and plucked and prepared them for the freezer. Also the biggest drake. Afterwards we took Bess for a walk through the bottom of Hayes Wood. She loved dashing around here and sniffing at everything. Fortunately she had just come back to us when we heard a crashing noise between the trees and several deer appeared, running just above us. It was exciting to see them so close. We held on to Bess and she kept quiet for once. She usually barked loudly at anything moving. The cats didn't often accompany us now winter had set in.

It was back to the decorating again, the kitchen this time. It was a large room and we intended mainly to use this one, because the Rayburn kept it so warm and cosy. It had a stone floor which Aunty Dolly used to wash over daily with a bucket of water and mop. We decided to fit a serviceable carpet, to paint and paper, to fix some new kitchen units and to remove any unwanted furniture. Iain put the units together for us and Raymond came later to fit them and change over the sink. The final effect was very pleasing. Now we had a warm, attractive room to sit in and eat in.

A large walk-in larder led off the kitchen. Facing north it kept food beautifully cool, making a fridge unnecessary, and our freezer fitted in nicely. Another door led into a spacious area we called 'back-house'. There was a sink there with hot and cold taps. A door at each end meant the campers could walk right through there to the toilet in the garden, without disturbing us. One day I discovered a woman, who had only just arrived, doing a load of washing in the sink. She had brought a large pile with her! I had to explain our water situation, also that she was taking all our hot water! Evidently I didn't upset her as her family came again the following year.

We only charged £2 per night for a tent or caravan. It was fairly basic, but in such a lovely position and campers were allowed to bring dogs and cats with them. One family, who came each year from Hampshire, brought two or three cats with them each time! They would park by a little beach and the cats would play there quite happily. They didn't mind the dogs and never ran off, which I found quite amazing.

Christmas was fast approaching and cards started arriving for Uncle Ken, some from abroad. We had never heard of some of the people and Uncle's 'address book' was rather haphazard. He used an old notebook so it wasn't alphabetical. Some addresses were written in there two or three times and his writing was not easy to decipher! I finally managed to write off with the news of Uncle's death to those who did not know of it. Also I sent cards that year to some of the campers in addition to my usual number.

There was a carol party at the village hall on 20th December. It was a jolly occasion and Raymond and Sylvia were with us. The following day we went to Maggie's for dinner after picking up my brother Ted on the way. We hope that he will be well enough to stay with us next year.

On Christmas Eve there was a carol service in church. We went on to Raymond's for supper, with other neighbours, Roger and Ann. Very enjoyable.

We went to church again on Christmas morning. People were so friendly, especially Mr and Mrs Williams. Once home we made the usual phone calls to family and friends. After our Christmas dinner, when the drizzly morning rain gave way to sunshine, we had a long walk with Bess.

Chapter Four

The New Year, 1987, started quietly for us. John Atkin was on holiday for about four weeks so we missed his cheerful presence in church. His sermons were always interesting and not too long. He invariably managed to cause a smile or two so that we came away feeling bright and uplifted.

A crow was eating the eggs in the hedge where a hen had been laying. We discovered another duck was missing. Had the fox returned?

The weather had become very cold, with a forecast of snow. We went to South Molton to stock up on food and we also bought a Calor gas room heater as a standby. Within a couple of days the snow began. It continued heavily all day and although it stopped the following day, there was a deep cover of snow everywhere, with drifting in the bitter wind. It was slippery in the lane so John decided to go to the shop across King's fields. He called Bess, who was slightly reluctant, and as they set off he was most surprised to see that Thomas had joined them.

Thomas was quite a large cat but he had rather short legs; the snow was so deep that it reached his belly, but he struggled bravely on. When the three of them arrived at the shop, Connie the postmistress took one look at Thomas and said, 'No cats allowed inside!'

We never knew if she was joking or serious but John told Thomas to stay on the pavement. He and Bess waited there patiently until John was served. Going back through the field they met a lady on horseback. She must have had a surprise!

It was still very cold the next day, but thawing slightly. Thomas went shopping again. No post had arrived in the village for three days. John was able to clear the lane a little and was glad of his new Ford four-wheel drive tractor. On the Saturday the three crossed the field again. John was able to collect our post.

On Sunday John worked indoors again and I made a fruitcake. Later in the morning we discovered poor Thomas waiting anxiously by the field gate for his daily walk. Of course, the shop was shut on Sunday and we had forgotten to tell him! He was glad to come back in the kitchen and warm himself in front of the Rayburn.

We were able to get into South Molton two days later. The roads get cleared more quickly here than they did in Chittlehamholt, which pleasantly surprised us. Next day we had no water from our cold taps because the tank in the lane had emptied overnight. Raymond came over to help John investigate and decided the troughs in the fields were responsible, so he disconnected these.

Raymond had a cow which he thought was due to calve. Because we had plenty of experience with cows he asked John to have a look at it. It was definitely not ready, but when Ray and Sylvia spent a night away John kept an eye on it, just in case. It was actually another seven weeks before it finally produced a heifer calf! I remember how anxious we were over our first calving.

We were surprised when a lady from Ford Tractors arrived one day with a questionnaire. 'I hope you don't mind filling this in,' she said.

We didn't mind at all as we were extremely pleased with our tractor. When she left she presented us with a bottle of wine!

Since the snow on 14th January the weather had been dry, sunny and quite mild some days. I was even able to dry washing out of doors. John made a start on the garden, ready for planting later on. He lit a bonfire which blazed merrily away – too merrily, in fact, as it set the hedge on fire!

'Quick, get a bucket of water!' he shouted to me.

For several minutes we were rushing through back-house to the lane, filling our buckets with surplus water running from a pipe there. Thank goodness we had water and that there were two of us. We were fortunate to put out the fire before it spread. The next bonfire took place safely in a field.

We pressed on with the decorating, upstairs this time. The two remaining bedrooms didn't take as long. We bought a new bathroom suite which Raymond fitted for us. It was good to have an expert neighbour for these jobs! He had built his own house in Bristol before moving to the country.

On 11th February, Catherine was confirmed. We drove to Nailsea for the evening service. It was followed by coffee in the vestry hall, where we had a long chat with the Bishop of Bath and Wells. He had been making the rounds and finally smiled at us and asked if we lived in Nailsea. When we said Withypool he became very interested. 'Ah, you know my second-hand car salesman, John Atkin,' he said.

We laughed. We knew Vic's family ran a car dealership and that he had been selling cars before entering the Church.

'He's a very good friend of ours,' we assured him, which was true. We thoroughly enjoyed our evening, even though we had a long journey through the fog and didn't arrive home until the early hours.

Thomas was off his food for a couple of days and looked very pot-bellied. We thought he must be getting food elsewhere. The mystery was solved when he was seen emerging from an old shed below the house. John investigated and discovered a small pile of dead rabbits stacked up in a corner. He had obviously been catching these and hiding them for his own consumption! John skinned them, cooked them and divided between the four.

A couple of weeks later we had three of the cats very poorly. One by one they started sneezing and coughing and had runny eyes, Pippa first, then Christopher and finally Jack. Thomas appeared to be immune. We asked the vet's advice as they became worse. He said they had cat flu and warned us that this was serious. He prescribed Oxy tablets and advised us to keep them in the warm. Unfortunately, Christopher managed to get out and disappeared completely for four days. We searched everywhere for him and alerted neighbours that he was missing, all to no avail. By the fourth day we had given up hope of ever seeing him again. I couldn't believe my eyes when, during tea, I suddenly noticed him sitting out on the windowsill as if he had never been away. By the end of another week all the cats had recovered, but now Bess was ill.

We took her to our vet in South Molton who, after examining her, suggested she might have been poisoned. We were told of someone local who had been putting down poisoned food, which had already caused the death of one dog. Fortunately, after treatment, Bess recovered.

During the cat saga, two of our heifer calves escaped from their pens, which started yet another hunt. They were later found in Mr Pershouse's field. At least all this excitement kept us busy and warm during a very cold spell.

Now the good news! We were able to purchase six good bull calves, cheaper than the last batch, averaging

£80 each. They all drank well this time. We bumped into Mr Miller, the vet who had treated the cats' flu. He asked what had happened with the cats and seemed rather surprised to hear they were all fit again. He said we had done very well to nurse them through the attack, as they could easily have died.

The hens had started laying like mad, twenty eggs a day. We'd lost our contacts from our previous farm for selling these so looked forward to the campers coming to help us out. Only three weeks to Easter when the invasion would start! In the meantime John Atkin took our surplus to an old people's home in Minehead.

We started to prepare Uncle's caravan for the new season and were dismayed to see what poor condition it was in. It had been used every summer for at least twenty years and always stood out in the field during the winters. We were receiving bookings for this year and realised it would have to be replaced. We saw one advertised in the local paper and hurried off to view it. It was an Eccles four-berth, very clean and had been little used. Also the price was right. It was slightly smaller than ours so we bought a new awning to attach to it. We moved the old caravan to an adjoining field and cleared it out. The mice had lived there through the winter!

One evening, when it was tipping down with rain, five very wet and rather woebegone girls arrived to put up a tent. They were from Kings of Wessex School in Cheddar, going for their Duke of Edinburgh award. It was a dreadful night so we insisted they put their sleeping bags on the kitchen floor and slept there. I don't know what the cats thought about having company, but girls and cats seemed quite happy in the morning.

George Burnell came from the village to look for foxes in Hayes Wood but could find no sign of them.

The lambing season was in full swing in April – later than on lower ground – and farmers were naturally anxious about their flocks. A second inspection a few days later and still no trace of foxes. We had no sheep that year so the foxes were not hanging around the farm.

Our family were here for the Easter weekend. They helped to do up the old caravan by repairing and cleaning it. John and Mike cleared dung from the shippen. Iain put up the awning on our new caravan. We appreciated all the extra help when they were with us. John rolled the camping field after first flattening the molehills and removing stones. I was in charge of cooking and house-hold chores, writing letters and answering phone calls. There were plenty of enquiries and bookings for camping now.

Maggie and Cathy came to church with us on Easter Sunday. The church was full, with people standing at the back. It was a fine sunny day and when we arrived home we found one family picnicking and others wanting to camp for the night. Next day three young men came to picnic and for fishing and booked the caravan for the first weekend in May. Our family returned home in the evening.

John Coe, who was arranging camping for Scouts, called to discuss this. He, with his wife and mother-in-law, came in for a cup of tea with us; they were very pleasant people. Just four Scouts came to camp the first time, and three weeks later we had eight Scouts and four Guides. They were no trouble at all and, since Mike was a Scout, we were delighted to have them. We were so pleased to receive letters from them later, thanking us. How good it is, too, for youngsters to belong to something like this, rather than hanging around bored, with nothing to do except cause mischief.

May commenced with caravans and tents arriving. Two couples, who had been sharing a large caravan, now asked if they could leave it for the summer months for an annual charge. They only came at weekends so we allowed this. Our own caravan was booked for the first time by Dennis and Luly. We had never met them before but Uncle had always spoken well of them and we soon knew why. They were a lovely couple. They became close friends, a friendship which was to last for many years, until both passed away. Dennis liked to stand on the stepping-stones with his fishing rod and Thomas would settle on another stone watching him. I don't know if Dennis ever caught a fish there – it wasn't the best place for it – but Tom was ever hopeful that something was going to benefit him! He also liked to sit by the fire they lit there. This was something that most of the campers enjoyed, as it was rarely allowed elsewhere. They found that food cooked out of doors tasted better, as we had discovered ourselves years before.

The day before leaving, Dennis presented us with a fine rainbow trout, caught in the River Exe. We appreciated this as the flavour is far superior to that of the brown trout in the Barle.

It was a little quieter now in mid-May, so we were able to go to Okehampton on the Sunday to see the finish of the Ten Tors. It was an enjoyable and memorable experience, watching the teams of six youngsters returning exhausted but triumphant from their arduous trek over Dartmoor. They set off early on the Saturday morning and the first ones started to arrive back on Sunday morning. As each team came into sight there was enthusiastic applause from the groups of parents and friends awaiting them. Although there was drizzle and fog on the moor, most succeeded this time. The year before, torrential rain, gales and fog all day Saturday had caused a poor result. We were thrilled when Mike led his team in and was presented with a silver medal for walking forty-five miles. The next year his distance would be fifty-five miles for a gold medal.

John was busy cutting weed in fields and rolling them when the weather permitted. It was very changeable this year: a few sunny days and then days with heavy rain. He also cut grass in the camping field with a hand mower, as Uncle had previously done! Not at all successful, so we decided to buy a six foot topper which, attached to the tractor, made a good, and easier, job of it.

Towards the end of May there were several campers in the field, including loads of kids. We welcomed children with their parents, but when many more turned up, just to visit people staying, it was bedlam! With balls and barking dogs disturbing the quieter folk I was forced to protest.

On our forty-first wedding anniversary Mike drove Maggie and Iain down in 'Bumble', his newly acquired bright yellow car. This was good practice for him in preparation for his driving test. He soon passed this at his first attempt, but just before this he and Brian decided to cycle down for a weekend. This was an eighty-mile journey and rain didn't help. Brian's bike packed up at Dunster so we had a phone call to go and rescue them.

The boys were staying in the old caravan, which was looking quite good now. Maggie had made new curtains and cushions after the painting was completed. It was certainly better than a tent in view of the weather, and they planned to do some cooking and be independent of us. They were in a field on their own and really needed a fine day on the Saturday. There were sunny intervals but also heavy showers, so not too good. Of course Sunday was dry and sunny! After having lunch with us they had to return home. Brian's bike had been repaired but we didn't know whether to trust it for the long journey back, so we put the bikes in the trailer and drove them as far as Highbridge. They managed all right from there.

We were getting so many campers and caravans arriving now that we had no trouble selling our eggs. Others were coming for fishing. People with dogs were finding their animals would not come past the farmhouse because of Thomas! He didn't set on them, just sat in the lane staring at them as they came up. Some were big dogs, including a rottweiler! We decided that they were so used to cats running away from them that they couldn't cope with this. Their owners were rather embarrassed and had to use their vehicles to get the dogs up the lane! This amused us greatly but we dared not laugh until we were back in the house.

On 12th June we had the result of the general election. The Conservatives won for the third time in a row with a clear majority of 102.

John did some gardening that day, putting in runner beans, tomato plants, sprout and cabbage plants, while I made an apple pie and seed cake. Next day John planted peas and parsley seed while I made marmalade and two rabbit pies.

We were overrun with rabbits. John shot two for us one evening and the cats were doing their best to keep them down. Not Pippa, who was getting rather feeble by then, but the other three regularly caught the smaller ones. We would see them pass the house with one in their mouths – always dead, as they would kill them instantly. John would hurry out, take them away and prepare and cook them for all to share. It saved on tins of cat food!

Chapter Five

With a good forecast for the next few days we arranged to collect Ted, my brother, from Bristol. There was no way of getting here without a car, as there were no trains or buses near Withypool. Also he suffered from angina and a painful, ulcerated leg.

We had to put all our work to one side while we entertained him and I must admit it was like a holiday for ourselves, driving him around the fascinating villages and beautiful countryside of Exmoor. He loved every minute of it, enjoying the wild moorland, the Exmoor ponies, the rivers and the coast.

One day we drive to Porlock Weir, via Cloutsham, Luccombe and Horner. All picturesque small villages, set among ancient woodland and mainly owned by the National Trust. It was a hot, sunny day and we were glad to get out of the car at Horner and enjoy ice creams purchased at the tearooms. We sat at a table listening to the gurgling stream and the birds singing in the woods around us. There is a pretty walk beside the water to Cloutsham, but not for us that day. We drove on to Porlock Weir and watched the tide tumbling onto the pebbly beach. A truly glorious day.

The following day we took Ted to the Valley of Rocks, one of our favourite spots. We drove via Simonsbath (pronounced Simmonsbath) up to Barbrook, Lynton and Lynmouth and on through the Valley of Rocks. The rocks, all strangely shaped, lined the road. Below the hills on the right there was a cricket ground, and on this Sunday a match was in progress. It was a splendid sight, the green grass and cricketers in their whites against the darker background of rocks. Further along we were able to walk the other side of the hills, overlooking the blue sea. Here the wild goats were scrambling about. There are so many here that they need to be culled from time to time. On a previous visit there was a large white billy goat who took a liking to us. We tried, and eventually managed, to photograph him, but he kept charging at us! I think he was only being friendly. Luckily they were not so close this day, as Ted was not too sturdy on his legs.

The next day it started with drizzle, turning to heavier rain all day. We just had a car trip around Hawkridge, Landacre (pronounced Lanacre), Exford and Winsford. At least there was little traffic about on such a wet day.

Typical of our English weather, the next day was sunny again, so off we went to Dulverton, calling at Tarr Steps on the way back. There were several people enjoying a walk across the clapper bridge and much to my amazement Ted was keen to go across, using his stick. I had no intention of going, although I had been several years before. For some reason I cannot cross over water without feeling giddy – unless there is a handrail! I'm just as bad on our stepping-stones at South Hill and usually walk through the water to reach the opposite bank – wearing wellies of course. It is not very deep except after torrential rain, and then the stones are underwater anyway.

Ted embarrassed me by calling out loudly. 'Come on Mary, come across with me.'

With many eyes focussed on me there was no way I was going to make the crossing. 'You carry on,' I said.

A woman standing beside me remarked, 'Your father's very brave.'

Ted is twelve years older than I am and I realised that with his grey hair and stooping over his stick it was a reasonable assumption. I was glad when we all moved off.

On his last day with us we went to Oare church and Robber's Bridge, in the Doone Valley. Another spectacular area, especially to anyone who has read the book *Lorna Doone*. The author, R D Blackmore, is said to have written part of this in the Royal Oak in Withypool. It is easy to imagine that the exciting story actually took place in the Doone Valley.

We took Ted home next day and stopped at Nailsea on our way back to call on Maggie. She had pansy and lobelia plants for us and picked us some raspberries from her garden.

Campers and fishermen were coming and going constantly and it seemed busier than ever. We had to warn women and children not to pick Thomas up, as they all fell in love with him. His beautiful eyes and his appearance generally were very deceptive, and the first aid box had plenty of use without him adding to the wounds.

At the end of June we had a good spell of hot, sunny weather and John started cutting and turning grass in four fields. By the fifth day he had baled them all. Raymond helped us bring in 380 bales for ourselves and took away 256 for himself. Not the heavy loads we had at Kinnings, but easier to dry and make. We continued cutting and did get rain on one lot. We called it spoilt hay, but the 139 bales were suitable for bullocks. One of the top fields yielded 207 bales and the six-acre field 140 bales of decent hay. John also cut one of Raymond's fields for him which produced 193 bales. We thought 1,166 bales very good for ourselves.

One morning we had a visit from Mrs Wilks of Dulverton. She had been a friend of Uncle Ken and wanted to meet us. She brought flowers for me and we had a very enjoyable chat.

A few days later Mr and Mrs Wilks arrived with a tent. They were not related to the Dulverton lady but had been coming to South Hill every year and were going to miss Uncle. They were an elderly couple and we were amazed to see them sleeping on the ground in their tent. They went to the Royal Oak each evening, sometimes walking, which was a considerable distance for them. Mr Wilks always brought a good supply of 'booze' – whisky and homemade wines – and these were offered to us whenever we had a chat with them. Very powerful they were too! They stayed in the field for two weeks, and one evening we invited them up to the house. After a short time, they tried hard to persuade us to go out to dinner with them at the Poltimore Arms, but we declined the offer. The food was tempting but not the drink!

David Harris often went to Cutcombe market on Wednesdays and would call in to see us afterwards. On one occasion he brought us 7½ lbs of blackcurrants from his garden and, another time, apples from his orchard. We had neither of these at South Hill so they were much appreciated. He also gave us the sad news that the lady who had bought Kinnings Farm from us had died of cancer and that Kinnings had been sold again, within a year of us leaving.

We were surprised to get Dutch walkers turning up to camp for the night. A few weeks later another couple came and the very next day a single Dutch man. Best of all were the couple who came and stayed for two nights. On the second day they decided to wash in the shallow river with the woman jumping in topless. We saw nothing of this but heard plenty from the campers! It wasn't that anyone objected but being something unusual it caused a buzz of excitement. They were the last Dutch people to come that year.

We had Bess very poorly again. The vet discovered she had a heart murmur and prescribed tablets, but these didn't help. One day she seemed a little better; then she was in pain again and wouldn't eat. This went on for three weeks until one day she was so ill that we decided, sadly, that it was kinder to have her put to sleep. The vet agreed there was nothing more he could do for her. We missed her terribly; the first dog we had ever owned and such a good little worker, and a friend.

A week of lovely sunny weather in early August persuaded John to cut another field for hay, as the grass had grown well there. He cut on Tuesday evening and baled on Thursday and Friday – 200 bales to add to our previous store, making 1,366 in all. We would have plenty of good hay to sell.

Maggie, Iain, Cathy and Denise came for a week, the two girls sleeping in the old caravan. Cathy enjoyed having a fire in the field and cooked sausages on it. One day they walked beside the river all the way to Tarr Steps, despite the drizzle. Maggie and Iain chose a sunny day for this walk: much more sensible! On other days Iain was busy cleaning the Subaru for us, as we had decided to sell it, and he made it look very smart inside and out. It sold the same day it was advertised in the *North Devon Journal Herald*, for a very good price.

John Peacock, a camper, caught three rock salmon at Minehead. He offered us one and asked if we could cook the other two for him. We were pleased to do this but, as we had our family with us, we put our fish in the freezer. Five days later we cooked it and enjoyed it for our lunch. It had been a hectic morning dealing with campers, and Thomas let us down by attacking Timmy, a Jack Russell, which upset his fond owners!

In the afternoon we went to a field in the village for the annual fête and flower show. Unfortunately, after an hour or so I started to feel rather queasy and wanted to go home. As we passed the village hall, where all the produce was on show, John insisted on going in to see it. Years before, when we lived in Nailsea, we both put in exhibits every year. Also in shows at Clevedon, Portishead, Tickenham, and even the big Bristol show on the Downs. We received a large pile of certificates to prove our successes. However, on this occasion I felt too poorly to stay and we soon arrived home, much to John's disappointment. Just the thought of tea caused me to vomit and within a short time John joined me! All that evening we sat, with a bucket each, a glass of water and paper tissues, and felt we were dying! It is amusing to think back on now, but ghastly at the time. We realised it was the rock salmon. At the age of eight I had suffered from fish poisoning and the symptoms were identical and never forgotten!

A few days after this I answered a knock on the kitchen door. Mr Fielding, a camper, handed me a small parcel, saying, 'I caught you a fish in Wimbleball reservoir.'

I managed to smile and thank him, although I had sworn never to eat fish again. But I did, and we both enjoyed it because it was rainbow trout – our favourite.

We had Mrs Hooper call here one day, with her family. She once lived here at South Hill but left forty years ago. Passing nearby she couldn't resist seeing her old home again. We remembered Raymond telling us he was evacuated to South Hill during the war, so I believe she called on him afterwards.

We were having trouble with sheep 'invasions' in a field adjoining Blackmoreland. Robert had bought grass keep there but unfortunately he lived at Allerford, which was some distance away. The hedge had not been well maintained and it needed just one sheep to wriggle its way through a gap for all the rest to follow, up to 100 of them! We had just lost Bess, and without a dog it was impossible to control them. Also, we had made up our minds to buy sheep ourselves so didn't want to see our own grass being eaten. Although we tried hard to block up any gaps, and Robert did likewise – sometimes coming twice a day with his dog – those sheep were determined to outwit us. It was a great relief when they were finally removed altogether.

Mike had two weeks' holiday. He arrived on the Sunday with his friend Stuart, just in time for a duck dinner. They decided to use the old caravan some nights for sleeping. Other days they travelled around, using their tent at night. Mike shot two rabbits the first night here. There were rabbits all over the place and they can eat a fair amount of grass. Stuart had to return home at the end of the week but Mike remained for his second week. He accounted for twelve more rabbits, going out with John each night. The cats were still helping out as well!

We went to a farm sale near Twitchen and bought a Vicon vari-spreader for £28. Raymond bought a tractor so was able to bring our spreader back for us.

Next day we went to David's, in Chittlehamholt, and collected apples, plums, pears and blackberries. He has a good orchard there and the blackberries are plentiful in the hedges. We miss these on Exmoor because of the beech hedges. These retain their leaves throughout the winter to keep shelter for the stock. They turn brown but remain until pushed aside by the bright green leaves in spring. The soil, sometimes with stones, is banked up before the trees are planted on top, giving extra height to the hedges.

In place of blackberries we have the whortleberries, or 'worts' as they are called locally. Bilberries is another name for them. They are small dark blue berries, which have one great disadvantage – they grow mainly on the ground! People can be seen on the moor, in July, bending over to pick them, a very tiring job. We were lucky. Uncle Ken had told us where we could find them in a hedge not far away, and we had no trouble picking them. I tried them in a pie, and made jam with them, but we didn't like them enough to bother another year.

So much was happening that September. We still had quite a number of people in the camping field, and some had come just for fishing. Andrew Snowden, whose house is between our top gate and the village hall, asked if he could keep his two horses in our top field and we agreed.

We went to South Molton store market and bought five Limousin steers. They were not delivered until it was almost dark. Harold Symonds and his friend came up from their caravan and helped us to get them in the shippen. Two days later we had an exciting day at Cutcombe, choosing sheep. We finally bought thirty-two Suffolk x ewes and a Suffolk ram – all two-tooth. We housed the ram separately until he was required.

We were having trouble finding a dog to replace Bess, but finally heard of a spaniel cross collie bitch, six months old. We called her Tess. On her first day she helped us to move the sheep to the caravan field, which was now vacated, and she behaved very well. She definitely showed promise. Thomas didn't take to her, though. Was it jealously or didn't he realise she belonged to us?

October had started and we were alone for the winter months. It was good to be quiet for a change, although we did enjoy the campers in the summer months. Many were more than willing to help move stock, carry in bales of hay, and so on. They evidently felt that having a 'taste' of farming is part of a country holiday.

We used to feel like this when we stayed with Uncle Ken years ago. I remember one instance when we moved some cattle for him. John was driving them down the steep lane from a top field; Uncle was by the house guarding one side of the lane, to encourage them towards an open gate on the opposite side. I was placed in the lane to stop them coming past the open gate. As they came into sight, running wildly towards me, I was absolutely terrified! I stood in the middle of the lane, arms out-stretched, with a stout stick in my right hand. They drew nearer, while I trembled but stood my ground. Gradually they slowed down, hesitated and finally turned aside into the open gate.

'Well done,' said Uncle.

'What should I have done if they hadn't stopped?'

'Got out of the bloody way,' he chuckled.

Now it was time for dipping sheep. Raymond had a sheep dip on his farm and Andrew took our ewes there in his lorry, which was very convenient. We took Rambo (the ram) in our trailer, to keep him separate. It was a glorious day, just right for dipping.

The sheep had to be pushed into the dip and thoroughly immersed, heads as well, to prevent fly strike and subsequent maggots. This compulsory dipping took place twice a year, in spring and autumn. The sheep emerged, choking and shaking themselves vigorously. Best to stand back to avoid a disinfectant shower!

Next, we had to get the steers in for worm drenches. They were no trouble, although we first had to round up three of our Herefords who we discovered on the riverbank.

The stag hunt came down the lane one morning. The hunting season was well under way again, after a peaceful summer. During the previous winter the followers had been driving their cars down again, ignoring the notice on our top gate, so John decided to place his tractor in the lane, leaving room for the horses to come through but not vehicles. This worked very well.

We had never felt happy about stag hunting. Being animal lovers it pained us to think of those beautiful creatures being chased for hours, with little chance of escape. At least the fox had a fifty–fifty chance.

Apart from the animals, we had cause to dislike horse-riders, who frequently used the bridle path past our house. I remember the day when Bess barked at one rider and he took his whip to her. Others insisted on coming through with their dogs, not on leads of course, despite the notice on the gate. We had to be careful now with the sheep, as we had no yard to contain them in for feet trimming, drenching etc. We had to fence off part of the lane between the house and the opposite buildings for this and hoped that nobody rode through at this time. We needed to close the gate in the lane above the house. We also fixed a gate to stop the sheep running down to the river. This caused considerable swearing from some horse-riders. One of them, whose horse wouldn't keep still to allow him to bend over and open the gate, whipped the unfortunate animal quite savagely. Is it any wonder that we couldn't tolerate such people?

One afternoon, when we were wandering around our garden, admiring the glorious autumn tints on the trees beside the river, we heard splashing sounds coming from there. We hurried down to investigate and were intrigued by the sight of salmon leaping in the air. They were on their way to spawn. It was an unforgettable experience. The females would find a gravelled area in the riverbank to lay their eggs and the males would then fertilize them. They had come, usually in pairs, all the way from the sea, and miraculously found their way back to the very place where they themselves were spawned. It was sad that only a small number survived to return downstream to the ocean once more. Some time later we noticed several dead ones lying in the riverbed, which led us to find out more about these amazing fish.

The tiny eggs may take many weeks to hatch and then go through various stages – elvin, fry, parr, and eventually smolt. These can then migrate to the sea where they find sufficient food to survive and grow large. One day, much later, they will return to their same river and the cycle will commence all over again!

We had started getting the field behind our house ready for the sheep. John was fencing and then painting the metal gates, and at the same time he also painted the vari-spreader, car trailer and our top entrance gate. I used a wire brush on the wooden gate and then creosoted it; also the stable doors. It was good to have the spare time for these jobs.

After church one Sunday, Betty Williams invited us to supper on the Monday. We spent a very enjoyable evening with Bob and Betty. Earlier that day we had been to a farm implement sale near Blackmoor Gate but found nothing there to interest us.

John gathered the ewes together, inspected their feet and marked them KB with Uncle Ken's marker. We then moved them to the field we had prepared. John then did the same with Rambo and put his harness on with a blue crayon. He also went into the field and promptly marked one ewe blue. When the rest were marked in quite a short time, we were pleased that we had chosen a good ram at Cutcombe. Of course, we would have to see what his lambs turned out like.

The family arrived one weekend in November. Michael and his friend Gareth decided to walk to South Hill, but at 10.30 p.m. we had a phone call asking Iain to go and fetch them from Taunton, which was as far as they could manage. He wasn't too pleased! It rained that evening and all night and with drizzle all the next day. Added to plenty of recent rain the river was well up and the boys saw a sheep being washed down. It was dead and the poor thing had probably fallen in and drowned. It wasn't one of ours, thank goodness.

Having already made two Christmas cakes, I was busy during the first half of December making two further fruit cakes, apple pies, mince pies, coconut cakes, a chocolate sponge and marmalade. Actually I have never enjoyed cooking. John does, so I am hoping that when we retire he will take over from me!

John and Raymond attended a commoners' meeting one evening at the Royal Oak. Certain farms were given commoners rights to graze a number of animals out on the moor, according to their acreage. This would not have meant many for Ray or ourselves but we had no intention of using it anyway.

We had a visit from a man from Nature Conservancy, wanting to designate our field below Hayes Wood as an SSSI – Site of Special Scientific Interest. It contained a large number of interesting plants and flowers, including orchids. We had to agree to certain regulations, such as not ploughing it up at any time, or cutting the grass for hay until after mid-July. In return for this agreement, which hardly affected us, we were to receive £230 a year. Very acceptable!

One Sunday we went to Exford church for a morning service. Geoff Scoins and Jill were there from Withypool. We were surprised when Geoff asked John if he would read one of the lessons at the Withypool carol service on Christmas Eve. John willingly agreed and was later handed a sheet showing the carols and lessons to be used.

We went to Maggie's on 20th December to exchange presents and for a Christmas dinner, and we collected Ted on the way. They were coming to us on the 27th for three days. We would have company on Christmas Day, as we had invited Raymond and Sylvia for dinner this year.

At around 11.30 p.m. on the 20th we heard voices below our house. It was very dark outside so we were unable to make out people, although they were flashing a torch around. It was rather scary, especially as we were so isolated. Finally they moved away. The following evening we heard voices again at 8.15 and this time John went out to investigate. He found two young fellows orienteering. They seemed genuine enough and moved on with their maps. We heard nothing more of this.

We had a full congregation on Christmas Eve and John read his lesson very well. Then there was a carol, another lesson, a carol and so on. After the service we went back to Batsom, for supper with Sylvia and Ray. Then on to Exford for midnight mass. It was a great start to Christmas and we made some new friends.

Christmas Day was sunny. We rang Maggie in the morning and then had Sylvia and Ray for dinner. Another enjoyable day, and we still had the pleasure of our family for the last few days of 1987.

Chapter Six

1988 started off with horrendous weather – gales, heavy rain and thunder. The river was right up, flooding the lower fields, including the camping field. The gate leading to the stepping-stones had only the top bar visible.

It was lucky that we didn't have campers in the winter months. Our bullocks were wading and swimming in three to four feet of water in the field below our house and we managed to get them safely into the shippen. Andrew brought his two horses down from the top field as we had suitable space for them in our buildings.

The whole month remained mainly wet, with the occasional sunny, spring-like day, so typical of our British weather. On better days John was cutting down trees in the hedges – so far twenty in one hedge – then sawing up wood for the Rayburn. All the hedges had been neglected so we had plenty of wood and he was now able to start laying the hedges. One day we had a splendid bonfire burning up all the odd wood.

People were already booking our caravan for the spring and summer. Neighbours were calling in regularly for hay, which was fast disappearing. Our own animals needed plenty while housed during this wet weather. The hens had started laying again, up to ten eggs a day already. We had no trouble in selling them now.

February started with stormy weather – gales, hail, sleet and snow. David rang asking us to go to a meeting at Liscombe with him on the 3rd. Fortunately it was a dry, less windy day. John went with David but I stayed home to cook roast lamb and apple pie for when they returned. David brought back our calf crate which he had borrowed earlier on.

We started doing some exciting alterations upstairs, with Raymond's help. At present the bathroom led straight off our bedroom; the smaller room, which we had previously converted into a bedroom, led into ours. We decided to build a partition wall, thus making a passageway between the two bedrooms. It was then necessary to have a further wall, at the end of our bedroom, with a doorway. Now we both had private access to the bathroom. Our room was smaller now but still quite big enough for a double or twin bedded room. Now we planned the other side of the stairs. There was a small bedroom here. Also a large bedroom where Uncle had fitted a toilet and washbasin. We wanted to enclose this and add a shower to create an ensuite. Maggie and Iain used this room so Iain spent a weekend fixing the framework for a partition, helped by Maggie. He then fixed plasterboard, with John helping, and then fitted electric lights to the ensuite and our corridor. Next time the family were down Iain fitted the door to the ensuite. The shower and further work would have to wait until the end of the summer, when we were less busy.

Maggie and I inspected our two caravans. Hers had plenty of flies in it and there was considerable condensation. It needed a thorough cleaning out and to be opened up on fine days. We had just enjoyed a good sunny week, most unusual and quite mild for February. Only ten days before we had had three inches of snow! Luckily, it soon melted so was no problem to us, and no walk to the village for Thomas!

My caravan needed the curtains to be washed but a couple of them disintegrated in the wash so I was obliged to make new ones.

John had taken advantage of the weather to finish off some hedging and to put in a row of early potatoes. He also spent a good time decorating upstairs; painting, and papering along the new passage. Meanwhile I was stuck with the cooking, as usual! This time making strawberry, raspberry and plum jam. All fruit surplus to requirement in the summer was kept in the freezer until needed.

We had a lady call regarding the Golden Horseshoe Ride on the 16th and 17th May. We had never heard of this but it appeared that riders would be coming through our lane. We thought nothing more of it, as it was some weeks ahead.

In the meantime, we discovered a hound chasing around the farm, obviously left behind by the hunt. He was very friendly and seemed happy to stay with us. We rang the Exmoor kennels who were quite unconcerned but promised to collect him later. We shut Tess into her house and the hound elsewhere, and waited for a considerable time. Eventually a man turned up. 'Oh! That's Fairfax,' he said. 'He makes a habit of this.' We hoped he wouldn't make a habit of it at South Hill, wasting our time!

Raymond had started lambing but ours were not due for a week or two. We were busy getting the barn ready for the ewes and we used hurdles to make cubicles for the lambs in the old fowl house.

Despite new notices put on our gates by the National Park ranger, to say dogs must be on leads, we continually had women through on horseback with two loose dogs. One swore like a trooper if we spoke to her about it. We didn't know who these women were. Certainly no one we had seen in the village, or at church, but we suspected they were in league with each other!

We were particularly worried because of the lambing. These dogs would run straight into the places we had set aside for the ewes and since all our buildings opened on to the lane we had nowhere else to put them. Anyway, one person we had an altercation with came back another day leading her horse and with her two dogs on baler cord. John said, 'Thank you!'

We had no more trouble with her.

I bumped into another woman who had just walked across the stepping-stones and entered our gate with four loose dogs. I asked her to go back and use the other path to the village, which she did. By the time the first lambs arrived we were having no further trouble with dogs.

The lambing went quite well. It started on 17th March and all but one had lambed by 8th April. Just one ewe had returned and her lamb didn't arrive until 5th May. One had aborted in February and four didn't get in lamb. We probably separated them from Rambo too quickly. We were pleased with him as we had fifteen doubles and twelve singles.

It was a chaotic time for John, out each night at 3 a.m. to check on them. He found one in trouble and had to put her in the trailer and take her to the vet in South Molton. It was a ring womb but the vet managed to deliver a double, the second one backwards! It was 4 a.m. when he returned to bed.

We had one lamb die so bought a tame lamb to put on that ewe, but she was stubborn and would not take to him. We had to assist to make sure he had any milk and when she continued to reject him we decided to take him into market. John washed the lamb with Fairy Liquid to remove the numbers we had put on each side of his body. We were amazed when the ewe sniffed him and immediately let him drink! They were fine together after this.

One weekend when Cathy was with us she discovered a lamb had fallen into a large bucket of water, and rescued it in time. It was soaking wet so we dried off the surplus with a towel. Once it had drunk some milk from its mother it was fine again. Cathy certainly saved its life.

As well as the lambs, we had campers arriving during March, and with Easter coming fairly early that year we were exceptionally busy. The weather was very variable and we took advantage of a sunny spell to visit Aunt Edie in Weymouth hospital. She was there permanently, in an elderly person's ward. She had just had her 97th birthday and we took her sweets and a bunch of primroses, freshly picked from our garden. She was delighted with these, her favourite flowers.

She was not actually John's aunt but his first cousin once removed, which always amused us. She explained that she was the first cousin of John's father, so was once removed to John and twice removed to Maggie. It was easier to call her auntie!

We enjoyed a picnic at Chesil Beach before returning home. All was well at South Hill, as Ray and Sylvia had looked in at twelve noon to check up for us.

After this we had three days of rain and it became cold and miserable. On Saturday, the third day, it was very wet, which was a nuisance as Mike had brought three friends for the weekend – Philip, Gareth and Kevin. They arrived in time to help us move some sheep and then went off for the afternoon. In the evening they had an inflatable dinghy in the river. They weren't worried about the rain.

It was dry next day, with sunny intervals, so they took the tractor to Hayes Wood field and tidied up the hedge there. This would have been helpful if they hadn't managed to damage the tractor door at the same time! Never mind, we gave them a good dinner – turkey, chipolatas and veg followed by apple tart and cream.

John took the tractor to be repaired next day. The door was easily straightened, for no charge, so Mike was relieved to hear that.

April turned out to be exceptionally busy with campers. Several were coming for one night only, mainly young people. Four Chipmunks arrived on a very cold, drizzly day and we felt so sorry for them. Eight East Taunton Venture Scouts booked in advance to come on 16th April, to camp overnight as part of a cycling weekend. On the 13th they were forced to postpone this as not enough of them were able to get the time off work. They hoped to manage it later on.

We were getting anxious about boys coming through on mountain bikes. There were bends in our lane which made it dangerous for people, or animals, walking up. They would find it difficult to get out of the way with the cyclists hurtling down at speed.

There were always problems with footpaths and bridle paths. The wear and tear was one irritating factor, especially as there was no recompense for this. Lack of privacy was another. Our path is just a few feet from the house so we got strangers peering into our kitchen and even having the audacity to wave to us! Others sat on the little stone wall, just outside, eating their lunch. We got bottles, paper etc. thrown into the hedges. Sometimes it was difficult to believe that the house and land actually belonged to us. Unfortunately, members of the Ramblers Association thought otherwise!

One day we were visited by a neighbour, who lived away from Withypool, but came to the adjoining farm for occasional weekends. He introduced himself and invited us to a celebration fireworks party on the Saturday night. John and I were not keen on fireworks, especially bangers, so we thanked him but politely refused the invitation.

On the Saturday evening we made sure our cats were in the house with us and that the bullocks were safely housed. Unfortunately we were still lambing at the time and some ewes, with their lambs, were already out in a field. The noise from the fireworks was terrific but it was not until next morning that we discovered the consequences. When John opened the shippen below the house he found it in a state of disorder. Obviously frightened by the noise, the bullocks had broken down their feed barriers, hay was mixed with straw on the ground, and the animals were still looking wild-eyed. The ewes appeared to be unaffected.

It was a pleasant surprise to receive a hill subsidy for our ewes. We couldn't understand why, as we had endured far worse weather conditions on our previous farm in North Devon, where no subsidies were granted. We were surprised at how well the grass grew here and were delighted at our hay crops.

The cats were still keeping down the rabbit population. Jack caught a black baby rabbit, his fourth in about ten days to our knowledge. He was not bright enough to take them to the back of the house but went past the front where we could see him and John could relieve him of them. Thomas was more crafty and we rarely saw him with one. However much they ate outside the cats were always ready for their tinned food, lights, and the occasional venison.

Thomas was proving useful in another way now. One day I was bringing the sheep up from a bottom field, hoping they would go through an open gate. I was amazed to see that Thomas had positioned himself in the lane just above the gate. The sheep were moving quite quickly but when they saw Thomas standing there and staring at them, they came to a sharp halt and turned into the field. It was exactly as he had acted with the campers' dogs.

When I praised him he showed off by climbing to the top of a telegraph pole, one of his favourite stunts. The first time I saw him do this I worried about him getting down and had visions of sending for the fire brigade! I should have trusted Thomas. When he was ready he descended beautifully, using his claws rather than falling, which I had feared. I suppose that living his first two years as a stray had sharpened his wits. He was surprisingly intelligent.

Following Uncle's earlier advice, we moved the bullocks to Hayes Wood, where fresh young grass had grown between the trees. Unfortunately, they broke out to join some cows in a nearby field. A neighbour alerted us to this and mentioned that he had noticed one of the steers mounting a cow. John, Raymond and Andrew brought the steers home and we shut them in the shippen. Next day Mr Wilson, our vet, came to inspect them and discovered one was not properly castrated. We informed the auctioneers and were pleased to receive, a few days later, a cheque towards the vet's bill.

Mr Wilson was very impressed with the Limousin steers and thought we would get a good price if we sold them now. We took them to Cutcombe and were well pleased to receive £560 each for two of them and £504 for each of the other three. Now we had only the four younger Hereford x Friesians left. Andrew took his two horses, Tingy and Nutkin, home. They were unlikely to be stabling at South Hill again as Andrew was trying to buy a farm in Scotland. We would miss him and Gillian.

Charles and Diana Anthony, who had previously been renting our caravan, decided to buy one themselves. It was arranged that they would leave it at the farm and pay for each night they spent in it. They came quite frequently and always brought us fruit or vegetables from their garden. We were doing well in our own garden now – when we could find time for it!

Apart from campers, we were getting lots of visitors. Dorothy and Margaret, from Portishead, spent a Sunday with us. We enjoyed a good walk around with them and moved the sheep and lambs to a fresh field. Christopher jumped through an open window in their car and helped himself to something edible while no one was looking. He was a mischievous Burmese.

Of course, our family came regularly. Not every weekend but often enough for Iain to keep our equipment in working order!

Myra came again for five days. It was showery most days but with sunny intervals, so we were able to take her out. We went through Cloutsham to Porlock and on to Minehead, where she found the shops quite interesting. We also went to the railway station to see the fine steam engines there. There is a regular service between Minehead and Bishops Lydeard, near Taunton, a journey of about twenty miles. It is the private West Somerset railway and the trains are often drawn by steam locomotives. It is a very scenic route, passing through ten stations, including the small seaside resort of Blue Anchor, and Watchet.

Another day we took her to Lynmouth and on to the Valley of Rocks. Unfortunately it poured with rain while we were there so Myra missed seeing the wild goats and had to view the amazing rocks – Chimney Rock, Castle Rock, Devil's Cheesewring and Rugged Jack – through the car window, which was disappointing.

Once Myra had left us we were back to work again. We brought all the sheep into the shippen, pared the ewes' feet and put all through the footbath, including the lambs. We were thinking of selling them all before we started haymaking again.

Our hay was in great demand, and with fewer animals in the fields we could make more. Also, with far more campers turning up and needing attention, we were finding it difficult to cope with animals, gardening, and improvements to the hedges and to our house.

When we discovered an ewe lying dead in the field one morning, our minds were made up. We rang the hunt kennels, who collected her; they did this with dead sheep and calves to feed their dogs.

Ray and Andrew helped us to load the sheep for Barnstaple market with the exception of the late ewe, who had only just lambed. We were delighted when the double couples made £118 and the single couples £86 each.

The following week we took our last ewe to South Molton market with her week old lamb. The same dealer bought her for £80. He asked if we had any more as he was very pleased with the other ones. Unfortunately we didn't. Raymond bought Rambo so we were now without sheep, so less worried about loose dogs.

In May we joined Maggie and Iain in Okehampton; our annual trip to cheer Mike and his team back from their Ten Tors walk. This was their final one, fifty-five miles, and they actually had fine weather for a change. Not perfect, unfortunately, as it was too hot! It was a long trek on Dartmoor, carrying their heavy packs, which included overnight tents. Kevin, Gareth, Philip and two others were in Mike's team and, tiredness forgotten, they were all smiles as they lined up to receive their gold medals. It was a great day for all of us.

Next day we had the Golden Horseshoe ride to contend with, at South Hill. We had not known what to expect, other than horse-riders coming through as part of the ride. With all the gates opened in readiness, the first horses arrived, their riders with large numbers attached to their backs. They rode past our house and across the river. After a pause when we hoped that might be the end of it, another batch arrived. Tess was barking so loudly that we shut her in.

One rider called out, 'That poor dog will lose its voice by the end of the day.'

The clip clop of their hooves went on interminably and there were about seventy riders in all. We noticed the same ones reappeared at intervals as we recognised their numbers. We never discovered the object of this exercise but were very glad when it was all over.

Exmoor is certainly horse country. In North Devon we saw very few horses and the hunt never came through our fields at Kinnings. Although we are very fond of animals, horses are not our favourites, although we do like to see the wild Exmoor ponies on the moor. There is something very special about these, including their rarity, as there are reputed to be only about one thousand in the world. They are pure bred and unmistakable, with their brown coats and a mealy buff colouring around the eyes and mouth. A sturdy breed, resistant to the harshest weather, they can be seen on Withypool and Anstey commons, Dunkery Beacon and Molland Moor. We often saw them on our way to South Molton. They should never be disturbed or fed by the public.

Chapter Seven

Late spring was the time for bluebells, and Hayes Wood was carpeted with them. They were equally beautiful, both in the rain or when the sun filtered through the trees to accentuate their blueness. We had to walk so carefully not to tread on them.

Going back into the house I discovered a young crow in our sitting room! The window was closed so it must have come down the chimney. It was flapping around and I couldn't bring myself to touch it, so John came to the rescue and was finally able to catch it and put it in the garden. Unfortunately it wasn't able to fly properly and Thomas suddenly appeared on the scene! I managed to lure Thomas into the kitchen while John put the bird on a roof, hoping his parents would turn up to assist. Later on there was much fluttering in the chimney and John had difficulty in getting another one off the ledge. It brought a great load of soot with it. He put that bird on the roof – there was no sign of the first one. After a considerable interval, a third one appeared with more soot. Surely it wasn't the same bird each time? That was the last bird, thank goodness. Just the soot to clear up now, which amounted to two bucketfuls. It had been some years since Aunt and Uncle had lit a coal fire here but the birds had now swept the chimney for us! Afterwards, John put a ladder up to the chimney to check if there was a nest there. There wasn't.

We were due to collect my brother again in a few days' time so I had to get busy cooking. I made gooseberry, blackcurrant and rabbit pies and a fruitcake. We liked to spend as much time as possible with Ted, taking him around Exmoor. Baking, washing and cleaning through the house in advance left us time to enjoy ourselves with him. It was actually a good excuse for us to have a little holiday!

Although it was June, the first couple of days were very chilly, with fresh north-east winds. We went to North Hill, Minehead, which is a vast stretch of moorland with views of the sea. On this occasion the visibility was poor, which was disappointing, but it was still a special place. There may be many people holidaying in Minehead who miss this altogether. At the far end there's a view towards Porlock beach, but not on this day.

We dropped down to the pretty village of Selworthy, with its thatched cottages and fine medieval church. On a clear day there is a view across Porlock vale to Dunkery. We were glad of a cup of hot tea and cake at Selworthy. We sat in a garden to have it and were entranced by a cheeky chaffinch, which flew onto the end of the table and enjoyed some crumbs. It was extremely tame and really made our day.

Dunkery Beacon is the highest point on Exmoor – 1,704 ft – with spectacular views. On a clear day, it is said one can see thirteen counties. In the past, the fire beacons were lit as alarm signals, and possibly for celebrations. We decided that Ted could not manage the steep walk, with his painful leg, so reluctantly omitted it from our itinerary.

Typical of our British weather, it turned warm and sunny for two days and then very hot for two days.

We went to Watchet and Blue Anchor one day. Blue Anchor is a very attractive name, although the place itself is somewhat disappointing. However, seeing it on this warm, sunny day, it was very pleasant. We were lucky to see the West Somerset steam train stop at the station to take passengers back to Minehead.

Next we visited Wimbleball Lake. This is the largest reservoir on Exmoor and popular to visitors for picnicking, fishing, sailing and camping. Surrounded by meadows and woodland, it is a beautiful spot, which we appreciated on the sunny June day. There is also an infants play centre and plenty of space for children of any age. Also walks – a rustic trail and a nature trail and the all-important refreshments in the summer months.

Passing through Winsford on the way home the car packed up! Luckily we were just near Winsford garage, where it was discovered the clutch cable had broken and would have to wait until next day for repair. There was no public transport to Withypool and Ted was looking very anxious.

'We shall have to get your father home,' said the garage owner, which caused a smile as it was the second time the mistake had been made.

Anyway, the wife appeared and offered to take us home in her car, which was a great relief. Next day, Charles Anthony drove John to the garage to collect our car, now repaired, and Ted paid the bill. We stayed home the rest of that day.

Another day we went to Coombe Martin and Ilfracombe, places we knew quite well but enjoyed visiting again.

That evening we discovered Tess eating something from a bag placed in a hedge in the badger field. She was very sick next morning. This was particularly worrying as our previous dog, Bess, had the same sickness which the vet put down to possible poisoning. Fortunately, Tess recovered.

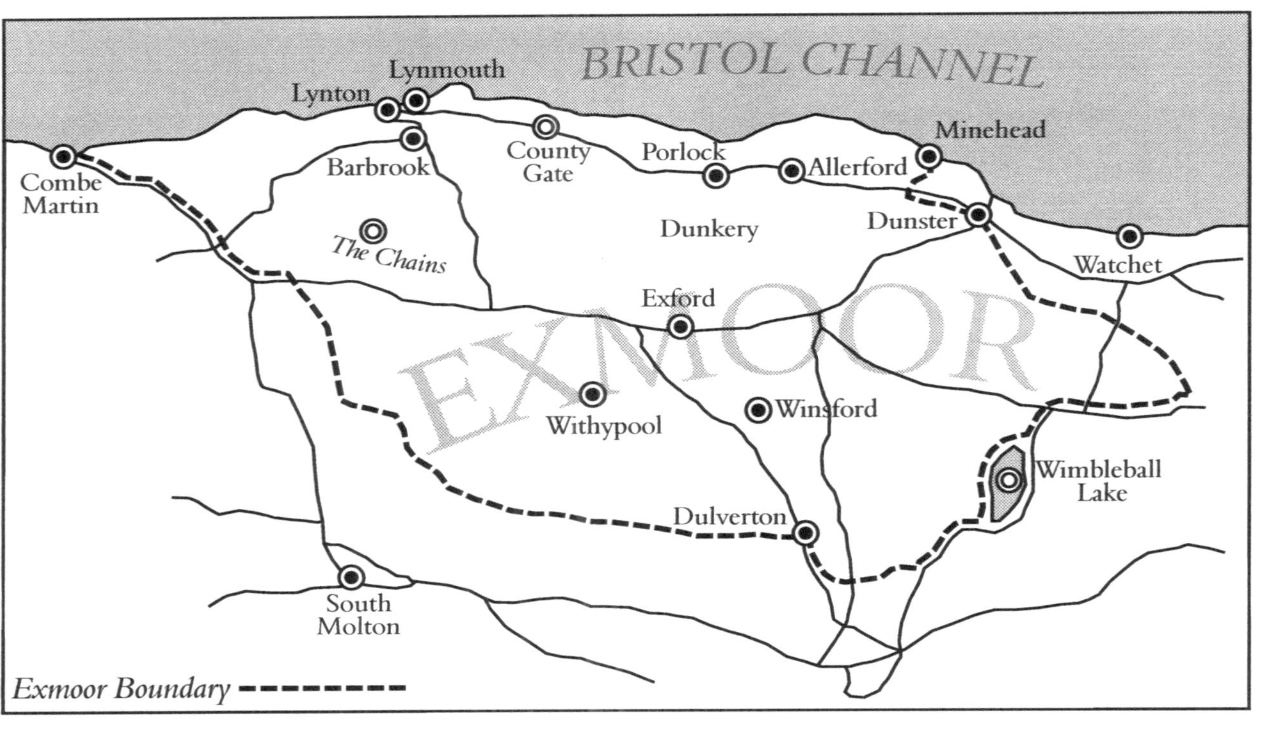

BRISTOL CHANNEL
EXMOOR
Combe Martin
Lynton
Lynmouth
Barbrook
The Chains
County Gate
Porlock
Allerford
Minehead
Dunster
Dunkery
Watchet
Exford
Withypool
Winsford
Wimbleball Lake
Dulverton
South Molton
Exmoor Boundary

South Hill, showing Thomas's telegraph pole

Thomas, who often climbed to the top of the pole

Below the house

Looking down to caravan field

John and Bess with the ducks

Enjoying the river

Thomas, Christopher and Jack

Pippa Puss

John tackling a very neglected hedge

River Barle in spate

Helping us reduce the plague of rabbits

Maggie with Bess

Mike, second from right, back from Ten Tors fifty-five miles

Cathy and Denise with campfire

The family around the campfire

First lambs ready for the field

Cathy with the lamb she rescued

Maggie at Dunkery Beacon

Dunster Castle

Dunster Yarn Market

Restored steam engine in Minehead Station

Combe Martin

View towards Lynton and Lynmouth

Thatched cottages at Selworthy

We needed to stay home on the Saturday, with campers leaving and fresh ones arriving, but in the evening we took Ted for a drive around Twitchen and Molland. Every road we took from here went through glorious scenic countryside.

We took Ted home on Sunday, after an early lunch, then went on to see Maggie and family in their new home – they had recently moved from a semi to a detached house, still in Nailsea. We were very impressed with it.

Now it was back to work. John decided to cut some grass for hay but the mower broke down! Brian Crook came in the evening to repair it so John was able to cut two fields the next day. The weather remained dry and sunny and three days later he was able to bale 444 bales of good June hay. Ray and Andrew helped to stack it in the barn. An excellent start.

July was a very wet month; a complete washout as far as haymaking was concerned. There were only three days without rain and two of those were cold and cloudy.

John took a chance and cut grass on 25th July but was unable to bale until 3rd August, that being the third sunny day in a row. It had not spoilt, despite the rain earlier, as he had turned it during drier spells to stop it stagnating – 223 bales. Another 309 were baled on a hot, sunny day and the very next day, another 315 bales, which was for Ray to take for himself.

It was early September before the big field could be cut for Bungy Scoins. It took John about four hours to cut the grass as it was very heavy and some was lying flat. He turned it regularly and it was baled on the fifth day, in warm sunshine – 745 bales! Bungy, his brother and Ron Fry carried them in. Thank goodness it was finished for this year, but 2,036 bales was a worthwhile result.

Returning to the wet July; we had the most caravans and tents we would ever have. There were fifty-four people here at one time, which was a nightmare, with insufficient facilities – just one toilet and wash place for them. Of course, many had toilet tents, and there were public toilets in the village. We had walkers coming through, some on the Two Moors walk (Exmoor and Dartmoor), and camping overnight. Several fishermen arrived. Considering we never advertised, it was amazing and could only have come from word of mouth.

One evening a family of hippies walked past the house and I saw a boy picking up stones and throwing them wildly around. I shouted at him to stop this and the man, presumably his father, stopped walking and glared at me, with a most evil expression. I was frightened but glared back and eventually they moved on. It was a nasty experience! It reminded me of an incident on our previous farm when my dog's barking had alerted me to a somewhat unsavoury character approaching the garden gate. I was quite alone there so I grabbed Bess by the collar and instructed the man to keep back.

'Don't open the gate,' I shouted. 'I can't control this dog and she bites strangers.'

Bess played her part, unknowingly, by straining at the leash and barking quite savagely. He muttered something, turned and hurried back up the lane. Actually, Bess was the friendliest dog, always eager to be petted and made a fuss of. She was just angry with me for holding her back!

One day a group of eleven, including two staff, turned up from an Ilfracombe school. They were to stay for the night and then walk on. The one in charge managed to cut his hand on a stone in the river and needed to go to a doctor in Dulverton for attention. While here, two cars with parents turned up to visit the children. Another two cars brought people to have supper with Mr and Mrs Gooding, in our caravan. Then a man rang to ask if we were selling South Hill, as he was interested. With everything so hectic, I felt like saying 'yes', but of course we had no intention of it. In a few weeks' time we would be quiet again until next spring so would be able to finish off alterations in the house.

Every day, weather permitting, I had a session in the garden; mainly weeding but also picking our fine crop of peas, or pulling the young carrots. All the vegetables were doing well. Unfortunately, I was being bitten badly as the humid weather encouraged the insects. On occasions I was bitten by horseflies, which caused painful lumps on arms and legs. The month of July is renowned for flies in the country. Usually we enjoyed walking up our lane and through the gate onto the moor, but in July we were surrounded by flies buzzing around our heads, which was infuriating.

Heather, ling and gorse were brightening the moor now and in our lane many flowers were blooming. The foxgloves were especially beautiful and many smaller wild flowers appeared in the banks.

John had cut branches from a tree to saw up for the Rayburn. A couple had just arrived with their caravan and when Mr Bowman saw John sawing the wood, he stopped for a chat. He was a forester – now eighty years old and still working three days a week! We certainly met some interesting people at South Hill.

We needed some more hens, as there was a great demand for eggs, both from the campers and from the village folk. We saw some free-range Warrens advertised and already laying. They were in Clayhidon on the Blackdown Hills. This was new countryside to us so off we went with two large boxes in the boot. We promised to buy a dozen birds for Ray as well as twelve for ourselves. We were impressed by the appearance of the hens and how they were kept. They were in a large grassy field, with several small houses they could go into. The owner had been selling eggs but the fox had been so busy there that he was now selling off a number of the birds. It was quite a job to catch them and as each one, or two, were brought to the car, John and I had to open the boxes quickly and then re-close them to save any escaping. We were counting them in and decided there were only eleven in one box so the man quickly threw in another. We settled up and home we went, only to discover that we had thirteen! We sent off a cheque for the extra one with a note of explanation. They laid very well for us and Ray was also very pleased with his.

Andrew had bought a farm at last, in Berwick-on-Tweed, and had sold New House. When they were due to leave, Gillian invited us to a farewell tea. We were quite sad to lose such good neighbours but they, of course, were very excited about the move, something they had wanted for a long time. We met the new owner of New House shortly afterwards and found him very pleasant.

Showers continued frequently throughout August. We had so many that year with tents and were surprised how many stuck it out. Several Dutch people had returned and our regulars were still arriving with their caravans. They often came up for a chat with me, mainly because of the weather and being unable to enjoy their usual pursuits. The entrance to the camping field was so muddy that we were constantly putting down gravel to enable the cars to come in and out. At least the field wasn't underwater this time.

We had a booking from a group of young men for a field, if possible, where they could put five tents to practise karate. We suggested a top field, out of the way of everyone else! It was the August bank holiday weekend and there was rain or drizzle every day. When they left, after five days, Tim said they would be coming again, but I rather doubted it.

Clive and friends turned up with a large tent for two nights. They stayed in the main field. When all these campers went home they left behind potatoes, which we ate, and lots of cakes and other food, which was a treat for the hens!

After the evening service at Exford we had a long chat with Vic. He thanked us for giving the silver flower vase to Jill Scoins, for the flower display at the village hall the day before. He also mentioned that Sally Page-Williams, Pippa's previous owner, was seriously ill.

Sally died a couple of days later; John and I went to her funeral at Exford. We were surprised to learn that she, and her husband, had both taught at Millfield School in Somerset. Ian Botham and some of our top athletes attended Millfield, a prestigious school where sport was given priority.

Our family were with us for the bank holiday and Iain set to work on alterations to their bedroom. We needed a shower in the ensuite, but the door leading into the bedroom was just where the shower had to go. This doorway had to be filled in and another one made further along the wall. Iain now cut a hole in the wall, and more work was to follow on future visits.

On 1st September we had very heavy rain. The river was well up and the whole field was soft and quite wet in places. A camper turned up the next morning and, to our amazement, put up tents. He then went home and brought his family back at about 10 p.m! They only stayed two days, although by this time the weather had improved. One day it was sunny and very hot. John and I sat on the seat in front of the house and relaxed. No campers and not a soul in sight! It was a pity in a way, as the whole week was warm and sunny, which set off several phone bookings for the following week. We did have two Australians turn up to fish but they wanted to borrow rods. As we hadn't any we sent them along the road to Raymond.

The hens' patch outside their house was so muddy we had to let them out by day into the adjoining unfenced field. We hoped the fox would keep away. When Dennis and Luly came the next week, along with several others because of the fine spell, Luly noticed a large fox near the fowl house. It was early morning so the birds were still housed, and so they remained that day. Dennis was fishing before 8 a.m., with Thomas in attendance. They both loved that cat.

'Thomas has no malice in him,' declared Luly. Evidently she had never received a bite or scratch from him!

The following week started off with a little drizzle on Sunday, showers on Monday, heavy showers and thunderstorm on Tuesday; however, it did clear up in the afternoons and the rest of the week was fine.

We went to David's one afternoon to return his sheep footbath, and had hoped to pick blackberries, but the hedges produced very few. Also his orchard was short of apples this year. Usually they were weighing down the trees but, like us, they do take a rest at times!

John took advantage of dry weather to top the lower fields. The topper removes the seed heads, helps to keep down weeds and generally refreshes the pasture. He also cut all the grassy areas in front of the house, while I had the unpleasant job of removing caterpillars and their eggs from the cabbage plants. Ugh! I later suffered from bites and a swollen knee.

Harold Simmons and family arrived. He farms in Cornwall but enjoys bringing his caravan here, by the river, for a complete change. Friends of his arrived the next day, their first visit to South Hill. Charles and Diana came for a couple of days and then were replaced by Charles's sister and husband. Another couple came with a caravan; Dennis and Luly were still here and fishermen arrived daily. It was like summer all over again.

John was now in demand for topping fields. He had topped some for Raymond, and now his neighbour, Ann, wanted two of her fields topped. While he was there, I had trouble keeping our four bullocks out of the garden. I was dismayed to notice that one had a torn ear, probably caught on barbed wire while escaping from their allotted field. They were a bunch of escapologists; however well fenced in they invariably turned up somewhere else, often in a neighbour's field, or in the river.

On closer observation I could see the ear was bleeding and covered with flies. I rushed to the phone to get John home quickly and we managed to house them and spray the bad ear. We invited Harold to have a look at them and in view of their behaviour, he advised us to sell them as stores. I couldn't wait to see the back of them but John, sensibly, decided that we should get the ear better first.

There was a postal strike during early September and Cathy was disappointed not to receive any cards on 5th September, her sixteenth birthday. These strikes certainly upset many people, for various reasons. There was a postal delivery again on the 15th.

Our family came for a weekend and Iain was able to progress with their bedroom. He moved the door to the opening he had made on an earlier visit. He finished fitting it on the second day, which completed his part of the work. Ray would now be able to put in the shower.

There was a heavy white frost on 1st October, which put paid to our runner beans and marrows. We couldn't complain as we had had very good crops from them.

Tim Hunt, who we hadn't expected to see again after the ghastly weather he had endured earlier, turned up with two friends. They intended to hike for a few days, leaving their car with us. John saw them leaving, all togged up, and asked, 'How far are you going today?'

'To the top of the lane, I should think!' Tim replied, with a grin. One of the trio was a girl and perhaps he hadn't much faith in her stamina. It transpired that one day of walking was enough for them. They returned to camp for the remainder of their stay.

Alex, Tim's bespectacled friend, helped us to find and return our four missing bullocks. It was their third escape in just over a week. We shut them in the shippen until we could arrange for them to go to Cutcombe the following week. The ear had healed nicely so, although we reluctantly had to sell them as stores instead of finished, we definitely had to get rid of these unruly animals.

Tim was lucky with weather this time, but after he had left us the rain and gales started in earnest. One morning there was a big lake in the caravan field, following a night of torrential rain. Mr and Mrs Glover, in our caravan, were quite unconcerned! Luckily, the sun came out later and the water subsided, but they did leave one day early, when more showers and hailstones arrived.

That was the end of camping for this year. Only our caravan remained in the field and Maggie's in the adjoining field. John put a NO CAMPING notice on the top gate and we relaxed!

We had two harvest suppers during that week, the first in Withypool village hall which, as usual, was very enjoyable. The second supper was in Chittlehamholt, where we had lived for fifteen years before moving to Withypool. We had a super meal, with entertainment laid on, and it was great to meet so many of our ex-neighbours. A very happy evening.

Now it was time to take the bullocks to Cutcombe market. John spent a considerable time fixing up gates and hurdles ready to load them from the barn, as arranged. We heard later that they would be sending a larger lorry so we would have to take them to the top gate after all. Raymond came to help us get them up the lane and they were soon away, thank goodness.

John followed on in the car at eleven o'clock but didn't get home until 3.20 pm. He brought good news. The largest bullock had made £530, excellent for a store, and the other three had made £475 each. We were well pleased with these prices for Hereford x Friesians. We had only two left now, slightly younger and well behaved. They had been kept separately from the others.

Later that day Sam and Rosalyn visited us, bringing apples and potatoes, and stayed until after 10 p.m. We found so much to talk about.

We had a day out, visiting my friend Myra in Somerton. She took us for a good walk around there, which was a pleasant change for us, instead of her visiting us each time. It is always so good to get back to Exmoor though, as nowhere else compares with its beautiful landscape and pure air. With more leisure time to enjoy now, we were having regular, local walks.

The family were here for half term, all doing odd jobs for us, as usual. Maggie was making a rockery in her own garden and we had fun finding some interesting stones in the river. She was excited to have just landed a job with Bristol United Press. Shortly after this, Cathy had an interview with Nat West bank and was told she could start any time! Once all four were working I hoped it would not limit their visits to us.

We were surprised when Lydia German rang to enquire about grass keep. The next day she and Percy came to walk round the fields with us and decided to bring over forty-eight lambs the same afternoon. A few days later they brought across over thirty ewes for the other side of the lane, so John used electric fencing to ensure they stayed there. We walked up each day to keep an eye on them and found the lambs very friendly. They looked in splendid condition.

Eleven days later they took the first ten lambs to South Molton market, where they all graded at 20K. They sent more at intervals, all doing well.

One day, a walker reported a sheep on its back. John righted it and it ran off quite happily. On our travels through the countryside we often noticed sheep with this problem so John would stop the car and get the poor animal on its feet again. If they were left, unnoticed, for a lengthy period they would die, or even get their eyes pecked out by a crow.

The hedges on the side of our lane needed trimming. John noticed Oliver Edwards trimming some on the main road and asked if he would do ours. He agreed, had a quick lunch with us after, then had a phone call to return to Westermill quickly, as a heifer had died and they were worried about her calf.

Next day we picked up a hen pheasant on the road, obviously knocked by a car, but not run over. We didn't fancy it ourselves but the cats thoroughly enjoyed it. The first pheasant we ever ate was a road casualty. We were driving along a quiet road near the Chesil Beach in Dorset, when the car ahead of us hit a pheasant and drove on. We stopped our car and discovered the bird had been killed instantly. We took it home, cooked it and found it quite delicious.

There was still a good demand for hay during November and December. Bungy was now asking about grass keep and later brought some hogs to the fields below our house, while Raymond put ewes in the caravan fields. All the fields in use now!

We had a shock one morning to find our garden completely bare! The sprouts, spring cabbage, purple sprouting broccoli – even the tops of the everlasting onions – had all disappeared. The ground was churned up and we realised the deer were responsible. Wretched creatures! Electric fencing proved the answer to keep them away and we had no more trouble from them.

There were two large-scale fatal accidents in December. A train crash at Clapham Junction on the 12th, when more than thirty people were killed. On the 21st, there was a plane crash in Lockerbie, Scotland, when 258 on board were all killed. There would have been many sad homes that Christmas.

Sylvia had invited us to Batsom for Christmas dinner so we went to Maggie's on the previous Sunday, collecting Ted en route. The usual happy day with them.

We had the carol service at Withypool on Christmas Eve, with John reading a lesson once again. The church was packed, as usual, with many having to stand at the back.

We attended early communion on Christmas Day and spent the rest of the day with Ray and Sylvia. Being football enthusiasts, we were interested to discover that Sylvia's brother was Phil Taylor, who once played for Bristol Rovers, Liverpool and England.

Our family stayed for the last few days of the year. One afternoon we all walked through Kings to post birthday cards to Ted. No sign of Thomas, but this time Jack accompanied us. We had intended walking back via the road but Jack led us into Kings, keeping well ahead, so we were obliged to follow in case he lost his way!

Chapter Eight

The first three days of 1989 were dry but dull. We set mole traps in the caravan field, assisted by three of the cats: Pippa preferred to stay in front of the Rayburn while she had it all to herself.

We caught four moles during January. We hate killing the little creatures but it is necessary as they make such a mess of the fields, throwing up piles of soil everywhere. We had a neighbour, many years ago, who caught one in his garden and was pleased to take it into the country to release it in a field. At that time I thought it very kind of him, but now I'm not so sure!

On fine days John was able to clear ditches and do more hedging, not easy when the hedges had been neglected for so long. Trees had sprung up everywhere, leaving gaps each side of them, the one advantage being the amount of wood he could cut out before laying the hedge. There was always plenty stacked in the linney (or linhay), beside the house, drying off in readiness for the Rayburn.

Our linney was stone built and open at the front, and attracted Hope Bourne sufficiently for her to have sketched it when Uncle was alive. Hope lived in a caravan, right on the moor, and had written books about Withypool and her life there. She was a most colourful character, and certainly talented with her sketching and writing.

Two days of heavy showers caused Bungy's wife to move their sheep up from the field by the river. She was very wise, as sheep have been washed away there in the past. Lydia's sheep had already left us for the time being.

On 8th January there was another serious air crash – on the M1. Forty-four people were killed and eighty in hospital.

People have already been phoning, or writing, to book their holidays this year. It had been so peaceful throughout the winter, as we had sent the occasional campers along to Batsom. At one time Ray and Sylvia had simply been doing bed and breakfast, plus an evening meal if required. They had a field leading down to the river and it was a great relief to us when they decided to take campers and caravans as well, as we were getting inundated here.

One sunny day John and I decided to walk a slightly different route. We crossed the river and, instead of turning right towards Tarr Steps, we turned left. Although many walkers regularly used this footpath we had never tried it, and it was definitely the last time we ever would! It was a real obstacle course: muddy, slippery, steep, deep pools to walk through and various stiles to climb over. I was exhausted on reaching the road and realised why so many preferred using our lane. Of course this was the winter time. It was probably better during the summer months but we weren't prepared to find out!

We discovered one of our water tanks had rusted out and had started to leak. Off we went to South Molton but could find nothing suitable. Brian Crook suggested Robby Tanks and they were able to supply – eventually! We ordered a 150 gallon fibreglass tank and were told we must wait for it to be made. Eight days later we were able to collect it from Chilton Trinity, near Bridgwater, and the following day we fitted it into place. This one would last for a considerable time – at least it wouldn't rust.

Now we were anxious to proceed with the shower for the ensuite. We purchased a shower cubicle from Payless and the following day a white ceramic shower tray from Gerald and Barbara in Withypool. Next we bought a Mira shower mixer valve from Plumb Centre: everything ready now for Ray to fix for us. This was finally completed and we were very proud of our ensuite.

Raymond killed his first pig for the freezer and we were having a half which involved sorting out and defrosting our freezer in readiness for it. When we farmed at Kinnings we had two large freezers, always well stocked with our own pork, beef and lamb and we really missed this. We have never experienced the same tenderness and flavour in meat since.

I noticed a recipe for uncooked apple chutney and decided to try it out. John, who disliked chutney, always complained of the pungent smell of it cooking so at least he wouldn't smell the uncooked variety. It was actually quite good, but I lost the recipe so it was never repeated!

I started making bread again while we were quiet here, using half white and half wholemeal flour, which we enjoyed for a change. On cold, wet winter days I didn't mind cooking. Back in November I had made the usual two Christmas cakes and also five Christmas puddings. It was the first time ever for puddings but although they turned out all right it will definitely be the last time. All that fuss – and steam! There are some quite good ones available in the shops, needing only a few minutes in the microwave to prepare for the table: much more to my liking.

The weather was very changeable throughout January, but not a single flake of snow. One day, after a heavy white frost, it became so sunny and warm in front of the house that I was able to sit on the seat for a while, accompanied by the four cats. John was busy hedging all day, but I didn't feel guilty as I had made blackberry and apple jam in the morning and cooked the dinner.

For the last couple of days Thomas had been suffering with a bad eye, closed up and sticky. When it showed no sign of improving we took him to the vet, who said he had an abscess. He was prescribed antibiotics and ointment and had to go back after five days. He fought over the eye ointment each time and I hoped he would not manage to bite John's nose as he had done once before. On that occasion we avoided going out until it had healed over, as it looked extremely unpleasant! The vet was very pleased with his eye after five days and said the abscess was clearing up well. That was a relief for John, but what amazed us was Thomas's behaviour, which was exemplary. No struggling or scratching when his eye was examined: just keeping still and quiet like any ordinary cat. He was certainly not ordinary. Later that day John was combing through Pippa's long fur, which easily tangled. The other three cats were fast asleep in front of the Rayburn. When John reached Pippa's tail she let out an anguished squeal. In a flash Thomas jumped up and leaped across the room to her defence. Jack and Christopher didn't even open their eyes!

We had a good walk around our fields that afternoon and thought how well they were looking. The grass had improved and the hedges were beginning to look like hedges, although much still remained to be done. Uncle would have been so pleased to know that we were tidying up the 'ranch', as he called it. The hedge trimmings, some from the holly bushes, were burning merrily away on our numerous bonfires. We were helped by a dry spell in late January and early February and it was good to be out of doors. One day we counted over thirty deer on the hill opposite. At least they were keeping away from our garden now. We had put a large clay pot and bins over our rhubarb, which was shooting already.

Lydia called in one afternoon to show us what a wholesale butcher in Tiverton had paid for her latest lambs, a very good amount. She stayed and had a cup of tea with us. We found the Withypool folk so friendly.

We had a visit to Maggie in early February, then went on to Clevedon with her, where the Clevedon Players were putting on *Adrian Mole* in the Community Centre. Cathy, our granddaughter, had arranged all the music for this and played keyboard, while a school friend, John, played drums throughout the performance.

The *South Avon Mercury* printed Cathy's photo and wrote the following:

Like most drama clubs the Clevedon Players are always a little wary when it comes to tackling plays with music. So when Felicity Peries chose *The Secret Life of Adrian Mole* for their next production from February 1 to 4 they showed more than a little concern when they learned the play contained 13 musical numbers. When the director discovered that only the melody line was contained in the script she must have had the first of those forty fits which seem to attack everyone who has ever been in charge of a production. Fortunately a few months previously Felicity had worked at Backwell Playhouse on 'Upstage, Downstage' with a 16-year-old Nailsea schoolgirl, Cathy Holland, and had been very impressed with what she had seen. And her confidence was not misplaced for, armed only with a tape of the London production, Cathy set about arranging the music for a piano, for rehearsal and with synthesiser and drums for the production. Just to complicate matters Cathy told me 'my piano wasn't in tune with the orchestra on the tape so I had to transpose the entire score.' Director Felicity Peries is so sure that it will be a success that she's persuaded the Clevedon Players to add an extra performance to the run and they open on Wednesday, February 1 instead of the usual Thursday evening.

It was really good and very enjoyable. We heard later that in the first performance their light bulb went out so she had to play in the dark until the interval, when the bulb was changed!

We saw traces of mice in our airing cupboard in the bathroom. This meant a thorough clear out. Afterwards John fixed gauze under the floorboards, hoping to keep the mice out. He also put a trap in but it was never used, so the gauze was a success. I only remember about two occasions when a cat brought a mouse into the house, probably already dead, at which I screamed so loudly that it rushed back outside with it!

It snowed towards the end of February, the first time that winter. It was quite heavy one day but it was soft snow. A few sunny periods the following day started a thaw which brought the river up. John was busy clearing out the loft and outhouses and I was busy making curtains. There was always plenty to do here whatever the weather.

On 2nd March we sent our last two bullocks to South Molton market. One of them graded but made only 102 pence per kilo. The other one, who we called 'Snorer', was rejected but fetched 108 pence per kilo. Quite ridiculous! However, they averaged £520 each so we were well pleased. We now had no livestock apart from the hens. They were laying very well again and there was a good demand for the eggs. With eggs and hay to sell, campers and letting grass keep, we were living comfortably.

Gerald, our friendly postman who lived in Exford, ordered 150 bales of hay. This led to other orders from Exford and soon all of last year's hay had been sold. This was good as John could now clear out in readiness for this year's crop. Some loose hay left behind was taken along to Batsom for sheep bedding.

Our first one-night campers arrived in early March: twelve Duke of Edinburgh walkers from Horndean School. Mr Folkes, with a broken foot, came in the minibus with his wife. The next day was wet and windy and due to recent rain the field was soggy and the river high. John had to tow the minibus out with his tractor and then convey the children across the river in the link box. Quite a jolly performance! They walked on alongside the river, probably to Tarr Steps or Dulverton, where Mr Folkes could meet up with them again by road.

We also had seven servicemen staying overnight for the Two Moors walk. A minibus and two jeeps arrived first to set up camp for them. The walkers left us next morning. They had been puzzled about seeing fires on the moor. We explained that this was swaling, a name given to controlled burning, used to clear the dead growth of ling, heather, bracken and gorse. This enabled fresh shoots to appear in the burned sections and took place in early spring before the birds built their nests. They were most interested in this, as indeed John and I were when Uncle Ken had explained it to us many years before.

Later that week I was taking in some curtains from the washing line when I tripped and fell heavily on the stone path. I hurt my knee badly and found it difficult to get up. I knew John was in the room nearby so I decided to stay where I was and call him to assist me. 'Help, help!' I shouted at the top of my voice. 'John, help!' No sign of John but three cats arrived, looking very anxious and pushing against me. It was so funny; I was laughing and almost crying at the same time! A few more screams for help and John eventually arrived. He lifted me gently and we discovered I had not broken my leg, just badly bruised it.

We took advantage of the quiet period before the main campers came. We spent an afternoon with David at Chittlehamholt and were interested in seeing the annexe that had been built on to his farmhouse. It was almost ready for Easter letting. We were most impressed and decided that if we ever moved back to the town this would be an ideal holiday base for us. We admired his calves and bullocks and then had tea with him before returning home.

On Palm Sunday we took some rubbish to Minehead council tip. The skips were very large so we anticipated going there again, having had a good clearout from some of our outbuildings. We walked along the sea front afterwards and were amazed at the number of people there, considering it was a showery day with only an occasional burst of sunshine. When we reached the railway station we were just in time to see a steam train leaving, pulling ten coaches. It was the 'Evening Star', polished and in prime condition, which attracted crowds of sightseers in addition to its passengers. We were told these engines were lovingly preserved, mainly by volunteers.

We knew that Iain was extremely interested in steam engines. The family came to us the following weekend and when we told him he was very excited. 'The "Evening Star",' he exclaimed. 'This I must see!'

So off we all went on the Saturday. John took two old water tanks to the tip in his trailer and then we gloated over 'Evening Star' again. She was in a siding this time, which gave Iain a better opportunity to admire her.

Early April brought cold weather again and even snow showers one day. The snow was worse in the north and one family cancelled their stay in our caravan because it was so bad where they lived. It was just as well as John discovered an electrical fault in the caravan. While he and Ray were trying to trace the fault he found a purse belonging to a man who had stayed the previous July! I rang his wife, and then wrote enclosing a cheque for £16.70. They were pleased, and quite surprised, but didn't want the purse sent on. We had two lots of boys turning up for fishing on Sunday. Two had no money and the other two were only wearing 'daps'! It was difficult but we decided we couldn't let them stay. We were getting serious fishermen here regularly who would not want boys playing around in the river. Also, if we let these stay we would probably get all the boys in the area down here. We felt there was somewhere near the bridge where they would be allowed.

We loved the Sunday evening service at Exford church and alternated it with the morning one at Withypool. There was never a large congregation at Exford: nevertheless it was disappointing to find just ten people present on one occasion. John Atkin announced there would be no sermon that evening, which was his normal practice for ten or less. This was a great disappointment as his sermons were always so entertaining, causing a smile and even a laugh at times, so that we came away feeling happy and uplifted. Quite different from my years at boarding school when we were marched to church, in crocodile, twice each Sunday – sometimes three times once we were confirmed. The sermons were long, boring and much dreaded. After leaving school it was many years before I attended church again!

On Saturday 15th April, there was a dreadful disaster at a football match between Liverpool and Nottingham Forest. It was an FA Cup semi-final being played at Hillsborough, a neutral ground. A large fence had been erected on this ground to prevent spectators running on to the pitch, which was becoming a common occurrence. Unfortunately, some trouble started at the back of the stand causing the crowd to push forward. Those at the front were gradually crushed against the fence with no means of escape. Pictures appearing in the press were horrifying, showing the terror on the faces of those unfortunate people. The final casualty figures revealed ninety-five dead and 200 injured. The match was abandoned and the fences on this and all other grounds were removed for safety.

It was spring time on Exmoor now. We heard the cuckoo for the first time this year. New lambs were skipping about, a little later here than in more sheltered parts. Cowslips, primroses and small daffodils were flowering in our garden and the grass was growing. Ray said a tawny owl was nesting in a hollow tree in Hayes Wood, with two eggs. The first swallow had arrived but appeared to be alone, although he had the company of a visiting racing pigeon. Nine days later a mate arrived for the swallow and off they flew together. The very next day 'Pigeon Pie', as we'd named him, decided he had rested long enough and also departed.

We rarely saw small birds here, probably because of the numerous birds of prey. The majestic buzzard, with its wingspan of a metre or more, was frequently present in the sky. We often saw one on a telegraph pole on our farm, waiting to swoop on some unfortunate small animal on the ground. Owls by night, sparrowhawks and kestrels were all on the look out.

We were getting very busy again towards the end of April. One Saturday night there were thirty in the camping field, including a party of young fellows in a white van. The Sunday was wet all day, typical for a bank holiday weekend. We went to a morning service in Simonsbath church which, to our surprise, was very well attended. On the way home we passed the white van with our young campers in it – they had packed up and left without paying. Luckily, it was the only time this happened. People were very honest and left their money in back-house if we weren't around. Also money for the eggs, which we always left on the shelf there.

On the Monday, eight turned up on the Two Moors walk. One managed to fall in the river (or was he pushed?) so we had to dry his clothes in the kitchen overnight.

We discovered Delilah, Ray's Jersey cow, in the river by the stepping-stones. She had walked through the river from Batsom. John and Raymond walked her along our lower fields, up the side of Hayes Wood and back home. Quite an adventure for her.

John was busy painting field gates, mending a garden seat and spreading fertilizer, while I was dealing with the dandelions that had appeared on the front lawn. I found the easiest way was to put a teaspoonful of cooking salt on each individual plant near the stem and when this reached the root the plant simply died away. Of course I always removed any flowering heads to prevent them going to seed.

We had some glorious weather during May and the camping field was full of tents and caravans. Two young men booked for one night only on their Two Moors walk but it was so hot and sunny they couldn't resist staying a second night. They were twins from London.

We decided one Sunday evening to go to Dulverton
church, as there was no service at Exford. We were very
impressed by it and stayed for refreshments afterwards.
Our vicar was there and he told us rather ruefully that
only three people had turned up for his service at
Simonsbath that morning.

Dennis and Luly were staying in our caravan again,
making a great fuss of our cats as usual. They came up to
the house one evening and watched a football match on
TV with us. They were a delightful couple and we could
understand why Uncle had spoken so well of them.

Our garden was coming on nicely, with potatoes and
peas well advanced. Geoff Scoins had given John three
marrow plants and Bob Williams gave him everlasting
onions. I love gardening but unfortunately the flying
insects love me and I am frequently swollen with bites
after a session in the garden.

All this hot, dry weather had come at the wrong time
for us. We needed some rain now to make the grass
grow, and the hot weather for haymaking. At the same
time, we had just fetched Ted to stay with us for two
weeks so didn't want too much rain for him.

We drove him to Tiverton one evening, via South
Molton, where we picked up the new link road for the
first time. We found it rather boring and Ted com-
mented upon the lack of scenery. We returned home
through Dulverton, where we ran into a terrific storm!
The rain lashed down, rushing like a river through the
gutters and making driving difficult. We were excited: it
was just what we needed. All across the moor it poured
down, looking likely to continue for some time, until we
reached Comers Cross when it stopped abruptly! The
road down to Withypool village was completely dry and
so it remained that night. The following day was dry,

sunny and warmer. We took Ted to Blue Anchor and, although the tide was out, we spent a pleasant afternoon relaxing there.

We did have some showers the next day but not the good downpour we needed. This was followed by sixteen dry, sunny days with the temperature reaching 80° F one day.

At least the campers were happy, and Ted enjoyed the warm weather and was content with wandering around the farm. He saw the deer at close quarters when a number of them congregated in the fields below our house. We took him for drives in the evenings when it was cooler. He enjoyed Landacre with its beautiful scenery and its medieval bridge over the River Barle. Although popular for picnics it was very quiet that evening, which tempted us to leave the car and wander around there.

Another evening we drove to Ilfracombe, which was experiencing a 'Victorian Week'. It was packed with people, many dressed in Victorian costumes, and a hurdy-gurdy (barrel organ) was playing at the pier end. We all enjoyed the exciting atmosphere.

We went to Barnstaple one afternoon to buy Ted some pyjamas. He wanted outsize to give him plenty of room and we had no trouble in finding the kind he liked. They were marked OS, made in China. I decided to swill them out for him first and because of the lovely weather there was no need for the washing machine. I filled the sink with warm, soapy water, removed them from the wrappers and plunged them straight in – which turned out to be a great mistake. After rinsing I hung them on the line, knowing they would soon dry in the warm sun and breeze. When I stood back and looked at them I had a terrible shock. They were different sizes! One looked very large, while the other was absolutely enormous. Now Ted was not a big man and only about 5 ft 7 in tall, but the legs of these pyjamas looked ridiculously long and the larger pair were definitely fit for a giant.

I wanted to show John, but he was nowhere to be found. I walked back into the kitchen, where Ted was engrossed in writing postcards to his friends. I thought he looked quite small sitting there. I tried to tell him about the pyjamas but he looked so puzzled and anxious that I burst into hysterical laughter. I imagined the little Chinese girls in the factory, holding these up in wonderment that English men could be this size! What if he had taken them home, unwashed, and started to put them on! I couldn't stop laughing and poor Ted couldn't see the joke.

Finally, John appeared and, after initial amusement, he suggested a solution. We sent straight away for pyjamas from a catalogue and these arrived at Ted's house a few days after he returned home. I was to alter the enormous ones to fit John! I took the scissors to them and cut inches off the legs, also from the sleeves and seams, and re-stitched them all on my sewing machine. A horrible job but I still had a chuckle now and again. I never washed anything new after that, without first checking for size and faults, so that it could be exchanged if necessary.

Chapter Nine

One day in early June two of our campers alerted us to a poorly lamb in Bradley Ham, which is the other side of the river opposite our farm. There were people walking through there with dogs, as usual not on leads, naturally romping around, barking and enjoying themselves. John decided to go across, pick up the lamb and carry it here for safety. He then rang Mr Pearce, who farmed Bradley Ham, and he sent his daughter to collect the lamb from us. People just do not realise the havoc dogs can cause among sheep, so they ignore the notices to keep them on leads. Mr Pearce of Great Bradley asked us some months later if we would like to buy some of his land, but we were not interested.

The lack of rain had definitely held back the growth of grass, which we needed for haymaking, but John decided to cut as the weather was so settled. It dried very quickly and didn't need much turning. The small top field was baled on the third day and produced 260 bales, which Bungy and Jim picked up and took away. Altogether we made and sold 1,664 bales from our fields, all June hay made in fine weather. John also baled another 667 for other people.

Mr Walpole and friends came here to fish but found it impossible, as the river was so low. Campers were delighted with the weather of course. Our regulars had never been so fortunate, with week after week sunny and warm. After dark, some people took blankets up to the badger field and waited there hoping to catch sight of these elusive animals. They only came out at night and I expect they were well aware of the humans around, as I never heard of anyone being successful. John had seen them a couple of times, the baby badgers dancing around the fields in circles. It must have been wonderful for them to escape from their underground setts.

We were getting a little anxious about our spring, though not unduly worried, as we had not experienced a water shortage in the three years we had lived here.

Towards the end of June we had a large number of overnight campers on a Two Moors walk. There were twenty-eight schoolchildren and six adults from the Rudolph Steiner School in Totnes. We wanted rain so badly, but why did it have to start just as they arrived in mid-afternoon and then continue overnight? There was a little drizzle every day that week: not very pleasant for them walking and not much help for our spring.

The following five weeks were mainly dry, sunny and very warm again, so we were still threatened with a water shortage. We decided to stop the camping, apart from our regulars who had already booked. We sent others along to Raymond who had plenty of water. We asked the shop and the Royal Oak not to send any more to us. People were very understanding, with the exception of two Dutchmen. 'We wish to stay here, we can manage,' they insisted. Finally, we gave in and let them put up their tent.

We were getting on in our garden where everything was flourishing this year. We were picking bucketfuls of peas and we had a good crop of potatoes. The runner and broad beans, marrows and onions were doing well, and for anything which needed watering we could use river water. Bungy had two cows and a calf in the field against the garden and they enjoyed watching us working there.

We have always found cows to be inquisitive animals and can only suppose it relieves the monotony of grazing or lying down to chew the cud!

We had an invasion of sheep around this time. Pearce's and Collins' sheep were the worst offenders. Pearce's were simply crossing the low river from Bradley Ham into our camping field. Jean and Frank Gooding were staying in our caravan with a very small dog called Tuppence, this being the successor to their previous dog Penny. They were very proud to tell us that Tuppence was seeing the sheep off! We were invited for tea and cake with them one afternoon.

Ray and Sylvia had a day in Bristol and asked John to keep an eye on Delilah, who was due to calve. She didn't that day, but the next day Sylvia rang to say Delilah had had a bull calf. They were so pleased that all had gone well. Ray had a terrible shock the next morning to go out and find Delilah dead! The vet confirmed she had had milk fever. We walked across to see them that afternoon. They had their family there, people in the flat and loads of campers, so they didn't need any further sympathy. A few days later they bought a Jersey cow, with calf, from Torrington market, so at least they would have the milk now.

Our elderly friends, Ken and Gladys Wilks, turned up with their tent for their annual holiday. The next day, at teatime, we had a terrific thunderstorm with heavy rain. The electricity was off until 3.45 p.m. the next day. Thank goodness we had a generator. When we walked down to see if Ken and Gladys were all right they were all smiles. 'We enjoyed the storm,' Gladys assured us!

We noticed a large number of children running around the farm, going into the fields and barns and generally making a nuisance of themselves. They said they were looking for clues – a kind of treasure hunt.

This was worrying when we had other people's stock in our fields and gates might be left open. We rang the Activity Centre to say the children would not be allowed to use our farm as a playground. They were removed and we didn't see them again.

In early July we had a large number of children camping for a week, from Withywood School in Bristol. They were very well behaved and no trouble to us: there was ample room for all their tents in the field as we were still sending most campers to Batsom. There was one incident towards the end of the week. Mr Furber, in charge, reported one of the boys had broken his elbow and needed to go to Minehead hospital. Fortunately the hospital discovered it was not broken after all, which was good news.

We were still picking loads of peas, shelling and freezing most of them. I was spraying the broad and runner beans for black fly, which was very prevalent that year. John was busy topping fields for Ann Jackson and Jill Stanton.

We had two more lots of Dutch walkers through who, like the previous ones, were adamant about staying at South Hill. We tried to explain we were short of water because of the hot dry weather. Also, that there was plenty at the farm along the road. They all said exactly the same. 'We want to stay here. We can manage.' We found it easier to give in than to argue! It was very likely it would be their last time anyway.

On our last visit to Maggie we had a good walk around Nailsea. When we had left it eighteen years earlier it was a village, but it had now become an interesting small town. Many new houses, shops, a large library, health centres, car parks, all of which we found quite impressive.

We always knew we would have to move from Withypool eventually, as I didn't drive and there was no public transport within miles. Because we loved living at the farm so much we had avoided discussing a future move. Now, suddenly, the idea of returning to Nailsea and being near our family again seemed very attractive. We realised we could have holidays again; something we had missed during our farming years. We looked forward to travelling throughout the British Isles, as we were only familiar with the West Country. It was exciting to make these secret plans; too early to divulge them, as we intended to enjoy one more year on beautiful Exmoor.

Cathy rang to let us know that she had passed grade eight piano. Also to tell us she had received two weeks' pay on her first day working at the bank!

We had an influx of people, luckily with their own caravans as they could cope more easily with toilets and water. The river water certainly helped out. Diana and Charles were here again. They invariably brought us fruit or vegetables from their garden and Diana would come up to the house for a chat.

Mr and Mrs Day came for their first visit. Their family lived in Withypool so were able to come to see them in the field. They were very friendly and must have enjoyed themselves, because when Mr Day came to settle up he kissed me goodbye! John pulled their caravan to Comers Cross.

John and Jan Joyner, from Bristol, came for two weeks. In the previous year they had helped carry some bales during haymaking but were too late for it this year. Their daughter, Christine, had been married recently and they showed us her wedding photographs. Christine and her husband turned up at the weekend and brought us some wedding cake. We were making such good friends with our regular visitors that we felt rather guilty that this might be their last time at South Hill, but it was too soon to say anything yet.

The Smees, Todds, Turners, Ovenstones and Browns were all here in the last week of July, all enjoying fine weather, although it became a little cooler towards the end.

Robert Williams called in to discuss his lambs getting through to us from Blackmoreland. Both he and John had spent some time repairing hedges but still they came. On one occasion just four came in so we managed to get them into the shippen, with the help of Mr and Mrs Fielding who were camping here. Robert fetched them next day and brought us a box of Dunster eating plums. Later on he brought us another lot. They were delicious and some compensation for the sheep trouble, which was particularly awkward with so many people staying here. We hated complaining to Robert but we had been told, when we started farming, that the onus was on the person who owned the animals to keep them within their field. I'm afraid the sheep found our grass more palatable!

On 1st August, England lost the third test match against Australia, thereby losing the Ashes also. Even had we won the fourth test, which we didn't, it would have made no difference. The only bright spot was Jack Russell, our wicketkeeper, making 128 runs not out.

On 5th August our favourite family arrived from Alresford, Hampshire. They were Mr and Mrs Flanagan, with their two daughters and four cats! They always brought their cats and this year they had an extra one, a pretty little ginger named Teddy. The girls brought Teddy and Totty into the kitchen, to show them off, while their parents and two older cats set up camp by the river. There was a lovely private spot at the far end of the field, where a small shingle beach was partly hidden by the hedge. The cats loved to play there. They had missed the best weather and had an occasional heavy storm during their two weeks with us but there was never a complaint.

At the same time we had the Rev. Andrew Matthews staying for eleven days. On the Sunday he and his wife went to the 9.30 a.m. service at Withypool, which we also attended. John Atkin had an 'assistant' – Lawrence Stanley, provost of Blackburn, who was holidaying at Exford. A number of Cubs were present, as well as many visitors. It was a most enjoyable service with such a full congregation.

Another camper, Mr Moore, brought us in a large rainbow trout one day. Two days before leaving he asked if we would keep two more in our freezer for him and he gave us two smaller ones for ourselves. We were very fortunate with these, one of our favourite fish, more tasty by far than the brown trout in the Barle.

It was the Withypool Show time again in August, and Lydia mentioned she would be serving teas at the fete. I made a Victoria sandwich and six small fruitcakes for her.

We had fifty-four of Lydia's lambs in our top field at this time, and Bungy had his lambs in a field behind our house. We hoped they would not be troubled by the invasion of other sheep which were getting in – or out – everywhere. We heard that someone was opening our top gate every night. Who? We could only guess! Diana found it open mid-afternoon as well and more sheep had come into the lane from the road. She helped us get them out. None of our campers would leave the gate open so it looked like somebody being spiteful. We were so relieved we had given up keeping stock ourselves.

Raymond put his lambs in Maggie's caravan field and Robert's sheep immediately pushed through the hedge to join them. There were so many of them, about one hundred finally, that they just barged through, making more gaps than ever, although John had spent a long time making it apparently stockproof from both sides. Robert and his son came over for the day and put up fresh wire, so we all kept our fingers crossed again. Jeremy, one of our campers, had helped us with the sheep at first. We had a good chat with him later and were surprised when Thomas suddenly turned up. Now Jeremy had a dog which hated cats, and plenty of growling ensued. Thomas evidently realised he had met his match and decided to climb a nearby tree, but not before he had drawn blood by scratching the dog's nose. Honours even! Unfortunately Jeremy had to cut short his holiday as we received a message that his mother was very ill.

We discovered some mushrooms in the fields by the river, the first we had seen at South Hill. Evidently the very hot weather and the eventual rain had caused them to appear, and we collected some for six days before they disappeared again. With all our own vegetables, plus fruit, tomatoes and cucumbers being brought to us, we were doing extremely well. In fact, we were giving away runner beans, marrows and carrots, as we had a glut of them. We picked the last of our broad beans and froze about 3 lbs of those.

Thank goodness the deer had left our garden alone. The electric fence had been sufficient, although we were rather surprised they had not jumped over it, which they were well able to do.

We had a hectic time here towards the end of August. So many campers again, also walkers and horse-riders. Grandchildren staying at New House were up and down on horses and swimming in the river. We didn't mind, for next year we would be the holidaymakers and we looked forward very much to that.

We were having some campers stay who were new to us, Mr Sims and Mr McCausland being two of them. Mr Sims arrived midweek, followed a few days later by other members of his party. Finally, when he was the only one left he came in for coffee and a chat. He had a look around the house and announced that he, together with Mr McCausland, wanted to buy South Hill. We were very amused by this and didn't take it seriously. It appeared that everyone wanted it, but we had no intention of putting it on the market this year.

John was fetching water from Batsom, about thirty gallons at a time, which helped for drinking water. Despite rain during August the spring had still not returned to normal.

Diana brought us a jar of apple and sloe jelly on her last visit, which reminded me that the blackthorn bush in the camping field should be covered in sloes now. I was right and soon gathered enough for making sloe gin. The sloes had to be washed and each one pricked. They were then soaked in gin, with sugar added, for a considerable time and finally strained off. I remember tasting it and John and I saying together, 'Oh that's lovely.' Then a gasp when it hit us! It was very powerful. Interesting, but not something we would want to repeat.

In early September Jean and Frank Gooding and Tuppence spent a second week in our caravan. When they were here in June they had drizzle most days, which was very unfortunate in such a hot, dry summer. We wondered if they would bring rain for us this time. They certainly did! On their second day we had a thunderstorm with heavy rain; John collected about eighty gallons of rainwater from the roofs. On their fifth day it rained heavily all day and we invited them up for tea and cakes in mid-afternoon to try and cheer them up.

The rain continued until the water came well up the gate by the river and the caravan field looked liable to flood. Jean and Frank panicked. They came up to the house for the night and slept in our ensuite bedroom. Tuppence had her own sleeping bag! Their outdoor clothes were strung across a line in the kitchen to dry overnight.

We remembered a similar night, several years before, when we had our first caravan in the camping field. The weather had been atrocious then and the fields looked likely to flood. Aunt Dolly had already rescued some campers and sent them upstairs to her spare beds. Uncle Ken suggested we slept in the loft over the stables. We took our two canvas sun beds, blankets and pillows and settled down for the night. It was amusing at first. When we tried to turn over the 'beds' collapsed, causing much merriment. In the middle of the night I was awakened by a strange scratching noise and then the sounds of something scrambling about in hob-nailed boots! I woke John who said, in a sleepy voice, 'I expect it's rats. They won't hurt you!' We were stuck there just a few inches from the ground, with these horrible rodents all around us and the rain still pouring down. That night seemed interminable but finally, at dawn, the intruders had vanished. Soon the sun was breaking through and we could laugh again.

At least Jean and Frank were spared this ordeal but we did feel sorry for them getting this weather on their holiday. We also felt guilty about feeling so excited ourselves about having real rain at last.

Next day the spring was just dribbling into the tank and the following day we were able to pump water up to the tank in the lane, so all was well again.

Later, we were surprised to receive an unexpected gift from Frank. It was a small painting by him of Withypool Bridge, which was very kind and most acceptable.

Meanwhile, Dennis and Luly had turned up on the Saturday, after Jean and Frank had left. It rained heavily most of that day, but the rest of their week was reasonable. Some days there was drizzle or a slight shower but it was mainly warm and sunny. They came up for an evening meal with us on the Thursday and we showed them around upstairs. This was to be their last time in the caravan, as we would shortly be selling it. However, it was arranged that they would come to stay with us next May, sleeping in our guest room. We all looked forward to that.

Fishermen were returning after a long absence. At last there was plenty of water in the river.

David rang from Chittlehamholt inviting us to pick apples from his orchard. He had a good crop this year, mainly of eating apples. We had a lovely afternoon sampling various varieties and gathering a large boxful to take home. He took our photographs in the orchard, with his collie in attendance. This was something we would miss when we returned to Nailsea.

Back at South Hill we were upset to discover one of Bungy's horned lambs dead. It was caught in the electric netting and John immediately removed all netting from the field. All the hedges were in a poor state here after many years of neglect, and although John spent a considerable time attempting to improve them he was fighting a losing battle.

Harold, Maggie and children, from Cornwall, turned up for their last week with us. It was always sad when we realised that we would not see many of these delightful people again. While they were here, Mr White and Mr

Snell took their caravan away – this time for good. They and their two wives shared a large van and had been leaving it here for the summer months. Diana and Charles also removed their van. Once they and Harold's family had departed we shut the camping field gate and the lane gates, and camping was over for good.

Chapter Ten

Now that we were alone we were able to make many arrangements towards leaving. Firstly, we had to sell our caravan, which was now parked outside the shippen. We emptied it, sorting out and washing all the contents. I was stung by a wasp during the emptying. Luckily I was fortunate to find a blue bag in a kitchen cupboard which, when applied to the sting, immediately eased it. This was an old remedy but blue bags were almost obsolete now, although used regularly at one time. When washing white items, such as sheets, they were squeezed into the rinsing water to accentuate the whiteness. Now, with washing machines and improved washing powders they had become redundant.

We gave the caravan a very good clean inside and out and were pleased with the final appearance. I placed an advertisement to appear in the *North Devon Journal*.

Now it was harvest time again. How quickly this past year had gone. We had the usual enjoyable supper in the village hall after the evening service at Withypool. John Atkin came and sat with us for a long time, telling us he would be leaving Exford Rectory and telling us about his forthcoming move to a farm in Withypool. He even laughingly asked John if he would like a job there! It was a jolly evening, in spite of the underlying realisation that we would be leaving a very special friend when we left South Hill. The following Sunday we went to the evening service at Exford, not realising it would be a harvest service there. John apologised to us for giving almost the same sermon as last Sunday!

We were so busy every day now, clearing out the old stables and outhouses. They were chock-a-block with very old rubbish, which we had never disturbed. Nothing of any value unfortunately. It involved many journeys to the tip at Minehead and we usually looked in at the railway station. The latest steam engine we saw there was 'Great Western 4561', ready to make its first journey from Minehead to Bishops Lydeard and back.

We managed another visit to Aunt Edie in Weymouth hospital. She was now ninety-eight and we never knew what to expect, but this time we were pleasantly surprised to find her bright and looking very well. She amused us by singing 'Good King Wenceslas' – a little premature as it was only October! We had a picnic lunch on the Chesil beach before driving home.

There was no immediate response to our advert for the caravan. The end of the season was not the best time to be selling it. We were surprised to have an enquiry from Hope Bourne, who said she would like to see it the following week. However, it was definitely a holiday caravan rather than one to live in permanently, so we felt sure it would not be suitable. The very next day a couple came from Yelland to view it. They had two young daughters so it was just right for them and they especially liked the awning. Because they had no tow-bar on their car we offered to deliver it to them.

Now we had the old caravan that our grandchildren and their friends had used. It had gone beyond any monetary value so we were relieved when Raymond offered to take it off our hands, as he hoped to make use of the chassis. John and Ray had quite a job getting it along to Batsom as one tyre burst and the towing bar broke en-route!

Ray and Sylvia had a few days in Malta, a birthday present to Sylvia from her family, who milked Jezebel and fed the pigs the first few days they were away. John took over the last two days and also cleaned out the pigs.

Bob and Betty Williams came in for supper one evening. We enjoyed their visit very much, and their conversation.

We also had a visit from Beryl Waldron from Chittlehampton. She was always interested in gardens but this time we had very little to show her. We had taken the bean sticks down, cleared all the summer crops and John had used the Merry Tiller on a good part of it. Nevertheless, the three of us wandered down the path and were suddenly joined by the four cats. To our amazement they started fighting, quite vicious fighting: yowling and hissing, with fur flying everywhere. We had great difficulty in stopping them, but they quietened down eventually. Beryl asked if they often fought each other. 'Definitely not,' I assured her. 'They've always been friendly in the three years we've had them.'

Pippa's behaviour was the most surprising. She would always lie contentedly in front of the Rayburn with the other three but had never previously joined them out of doors. She was quite elderly now and had seemed very feeble in recent weeks, so it was amazing to see her so 'fighting fit' in the garden. It wasn't to last however. She deteriorated rapidly in the following days and one morning we found her stumbling about, bumping into furniture and very weak. It was a sunny morning so John took her out onto the garden path. She stayed quite still and shortly afterwards she died there, in the same spot. Poor little Pippa. I think she had been happy with us.

Next time our family arrived for a weekend they brought a cat with them! It was a pure white cat, named

Binky, a rescue cat which they had adopted from a local charity. I don't think Binky really enjoyed it here, as she didn't take to our cats.

On 29th October we had about fifty horse-riders through our farm. We didn't mind that as it was a sponsored ride for the Macmillan Cancer Fund and we had received prior notice of it. It was a terrible day. Following heavy gales overnight, the strong winds and heavy rain continued throughout the day. Such a shame as the next day was dry, sunny and warm.

In early November we had more bonfires and the empty pole barn (for hay) which the recent gales had played havoc with, had to be dismantled. Some of the wood was useful for our Rayburn but there was a certain amount of rubbish to be burnt outside. We started a good bonfire but the wind invariably blew the smoke towards the lane where we were working. It is a strange thing with bonfires that wherever you move to get away from the smoke, it always follows you about!

It was just our luck that two people on horseback chose this time to come through. The horses simply refused to come past the smoke. When gentle persuasion failed, stronger measures were used and eventually they went on, with sour looks for us from their owners. John told me of a previous occasion when Michael was using the strimmer on the grass around the barn. Horses came down then and didn't like the noise. The riders were quite abusive towards Michael, shouting at him to stop. John told him to carry on! So they didn't like the smoke, didn't like the noise, didn't like our dog barking. What would it be next?

The same day as the smoke fiasco a party of young people walked down to cross the river. The water was partly covering the stepping-stones, making them quite slippery. They had to take off their wellies, their socks and even their trousers to walk through the water! At least we couldn't be blamed for that.

On Remembrance Sunday we decided to go to the evening service at Exford, as we were busy gardening in the morning. It was the usual fortnightly service there so we were surprised on our arrival to meet John Atkin on his way out. 'Oh do come in,' he said. 'We had our service this morning, but you are very welcome.'

We hadn't heard of this alteration for Remembrance Sunday so feeling rather foolish we turned to go out, assuring him it was our mistake. 'No,' he insisted. 'You have come and we shall have a service.' Indeed we did!

It was certainly strange with just the two of us and no organ or hymns. Vic conducted the service from the prayer book, standing beside us, and with he and John reading the lessons. It seemed unreal, yet very fulfilling, something we would never forget.

He had probably been looking forward to a pleasant, relaxed evening but he showed no signs of it. In fact he gave us the impression that we were doing him a favour rather than the other way round.

The days sped by. The clearing out seemed endless and involved so many journeys to the tip, either at Minehead or Brushford. We killed off more hens, and plucked and froze them, as many had stopped laying for the winter months and would serve better as meals for us. We were then able to clean out part of their housing, the shippen, the loft and other outbuildings. The latter were littered with items, some having been there for very many years. They needed careful sorting through before disposal. It was a dusty job but after sweeping and washing down inside the buildings the result was very gratifying.

In the house I was sorting through the well-packed freezer. Much of the lovely fruit we had collected during the summer I made into jam or pies. It would have to be used up during the next five or six months, as we wouldn't be needing this large freezer when we moved.

One Sunday we walked through Hayes Wood to Raymond's field to see the huge tree in the river which we heard had come down in the recent gales. Thomas came all the way with us and was very put out when Jezebel, the cow, chased him. He must have been in shock afterwards because when he ran into Sylvia's kitchen and she lifted him up and put him outside, he made no protest. She was very lucky. Thomas hated being picked up and usually scratched or bit.

We decided to walk back along the road. It was quiet there until someone suddenly appeared in the distance with two dogs. We were afraid Thomas might confront them as they were coming up the hill. There was a van parked on the side of the road, and to our great relief Thomas slid underneath it until the dogs passed by without seeing him.

On 21st November we watched the TV coverage of the House of Commons. It was the first time on television and we found it quite entertaining.

My brother Ted had been in hospital, in Bristol, for several days and we had made a couple of visits to his house to clean and tidy up and do washing for him. We had a letter from him with strict instructions, for the second time, not to visit him in hospital.

At our farm, Bungy was taking his sheep out and a few days later he took away his two cows and Bully. Bully went off to market.

Lydia brought back her sheep, which had gone home earlier for dipping and other attention. There had been no other sheep breaking in recently so we hoped she and Percy would not have any further trouble, as they were such a very nice couple. All was well for about three weeks. Then in came about twenty ewes, belonging to the Branfields of Hawkridge. This was a new name to us. We rang Mrs Branfield and they were quickly removed.

Our television set was on the blink. John decided the aerial was at fault, possibly because of the very strong winds we were getting. He tried to correct it without success, even though he cut down tree branches from around the aerial in case they were interfering with it. We sent for Mr Stoneman of Witheridge, but he could only manage a temporary job until after Christmas.

On 20th December John complained of feeling poorly. Two days later he felt ill enough to stay in bed for the day, most unusual for him. I walked down to the shop and told Jill he wouldn't be able to read the lesson at the carol service on Sunday. We realised he had flu and by that evening I, also, had gone down with it.

Our neighbours were very kind. Lydia fetched the local paper for us on the Saturday. We found milk and a present from Sylvia in back-house. Also a card and chocolates from Bungy and Shirley, who we later heard also had flu, as had Ann Jackson and another neighbour, Mr Hobson. We remained in isolation for a few days as we didn't want to pass it on.

Christmas Eve was the most horrible day, with severe gales and heavy rain throughout. John had started the day feeling somewhat better, but having to chase more sheep out and replace some slates on the roof in all that terrible weather, he felt rotten again by the evening.

Christmas day was calmer but we didn't feel too good and couldn't face a turkey dinner. We hoped we might manage it on Boxing Day. This turned out to be sunny after a ground frost, so we managed a little walk by the river, thinking it might improve our appetites. We met Dr Payne from Kings who had come over to wish us a Happy New Year!

We could only eat very small portions of food and fancied mashed bananas for afters rather than Christmas pudding! What a strange Christmas it had been. Perhaps it was just as well, as we were unlikely to be looking back at it with nostalgia. Instead, we hoped to be settled back in Nailsea next Christmas with our family around us.

We had just about recovered by 31st December. Our appetites had improved and we managed a good walk in the afternoon.

Chapter Eleven

January 1990 was a mixed month in every way, including the weather. We had a few lovely sunny days but many were wet with torrential rain at times. It snowed on two days but this was quickly dispersed by the heavy rain. The month ended with terrific gales – more news of that later.

We had kept away from people, including Ray and Sylvia, while we had flu. We eventually phoned them only to learn that they had also succumbed to it since Christmas and were still feeling poorly.

We were feeling quite well again, able to shop in South Molton and to go to Dulverton library for some books. I also started a jigsaw puzzle. We didn't expect to do much work outside this month but unexpected news of Ted gave us plenty to do in Bristol.

He was still in hospital there. Apart from the leg ulcers he had suffered from for some time he now had angina, fluid on the lungs and prostrate trouble. He was now feeling frightened and quite anxious to see us. When we arrived at the hospital there was talk of him applying for sheltered housing, as there was no possibility of him living alone in his own house. It was made clear that his house would have to be sold to pay for his keep in the home.

Apart from this being upsetting for Ted, it was also a shock to us. It was bad enough to have the trauma of selling South Hill without the prospect of selling a house in Bristol as well. We anticipated with dread the many necessary journeys backwards and forwards.

Our first visit was to sort out the food in his kitchen. He had been in hospital for such a long time that several items were past their sell-by date and needed to be thrown out. The rest we took home with us. We cleaned out the kitchen cabinet, dresser and gas cooker, and then stopped at the hospital to see Ted.

The weather was appalling. The terrible gales and heavy rain overnight had actually increased during the day. When we left the hospital we were amazed to see that a huge tree had fallen, quite near to where we had parked the car. That was the beginning of a nightmare journey home. It took us four and a half hours, during which time we counted twenty-seven big trees down, some just being removed from the road, and three large lorries and one van which had overturned. The M5 motorway was closed that afternoon and all traffic was using the A38, nose to tail, and moving very slowly. With hailstones beating against the windscreen at times, it was a terrifying journey.

When we finally arrived at South Hill we had to remove several branches from our lane before we could drive down. At least we were safe! We heard next day that there was terrible damage throughout the country, forty-five people had been killed and many homes were without electricity. Next morning we had a thin layer of snow first thing and several wintry showers throughout the day, but heavy rain gradually cleared this away.

We discovered later that three galvanised sheets had blown off the shed in our top field, so John had to retrieve these and fix them again. He then borrowed a long ladder from Raymond and spent most of a day on the shippen roof, reinforcing it against further threatened gales. It was no surprise to find our phone out of order. Later, Ray came to help with repairs to the end of the shippen roof.

In early February we visited Ted's home again, this

time to collect all his clothing, bed linen etc, leaving his wardrobe and bedroom cupboards empty. Then the family arrived at the weekend to cheer us up. First, Maggie and Iain, Cathy and Binky turned up, followed by Mike and a friend. During that weekend we had more strong gales and heavy rain, thunder and lightning, hailstones and a light covering of snow! They were lucky to get home on Sunday afternoon before the M5 closed again. There were many more trees down.

We did an enormous amount of washing, having Ted's in addition to our own, and took other clothes for dry cleaning. Some good drying weather would have helped, but we had three more days of rain instead. At last there was a fine sunny day, and I was able to wash Ted's blankets and raincoat. With that drying on the line we went for a walk through Hayes Wood with Thomas and Christopher. Several large trees had fallen in the recent gales, making walking difficult, especially with everything so wet. We made plans, with the sun shining quite warmly on us, to make the most of fine days in our remaining weeks or months here. We would enjoy the splendours of Exmoor, either revisiting our favourite haunts or seeking out new ones.

We were informed that there was a vacancy for Ted in Broomhill elderly persons home. It was in a district he knew and liked so he was soon settled there. We collected him one day and took him to his house to sort out his personal belongings and books. Rather a sad but necessary occasion. Next we had to arrange for the sale of some of his furniture and we took other items such as 'family heirlooms' home in our trailer. We then put his house in the hands of an estate agent and waited. It soon sold so Ted was all right for money and we had one house settled. Ours could wait for a while.

There was more terrible weather towards the end of February. The gales kept us awake at night and more trees came down, including six in Kings Drive. We walked up our lane and it was so windy at the top we were glad to return to the shelter of our house.

John was surprised to receive a letter inviting him to put his name forward for the Church Council. He would certainly have considered this had we been staying here but he had to reply explaining why he couldn't.

We were disappointed to receive a letter from Luly cancelling their weekend with us. She and Dennis were just getting over flu and felt unwell. Also they had an appointment for a new job in three days' time. If successful they might have to start straight away. It transpired that they did get the job, so it was farewell to Withypool for them. However, we remained good friends and we were able to visit them much later.

We were going to miss our evening services at Exford church. We had a most interesting one in early March when Vicar announced that instead of a sermon he would tell us a story about Cutcombe Church – St John the Evangelist. It had been arranged for the Bishop of Bath and Wells to visit there one Sunday evening. Unfortunately it was a moonless night and his driver drove round and round but could not find the way. They expected to find a church lit up and ready to welcome them but everything was quiet and very dark. Finally they had to enquire at a pub for directions.

Meanwhile there was panic at the church as there had been a sudden power cut. An expectant congregation had gathered but there was no electric lighting or organ. It couldn't have happened at a worse time. A few candles helped to improve the complete darkness. Then a local farmer suggested fetching his standby generator, driven by a tractor, and two men left the church to collect this. It all took some time but eventually the church was illuminated and the bishop finally able to discover it and go in. Shortly afterwards the power was on again and everything back to normal. Did the bishop have a word with 'One above', we wondered!

John Atkin recounted this in such a way that we were soon smiling and finally laughing. He had a wonderful way with words and he reminded me of my father who had had a similar gift. When I was a child he could change my tears to laughter in just a few seconds and always made the most mundane thing sound amusing.

We now had a whole week in March with warm, sunny weather, so we took advantage of this for some sightseeing on Exmoor. The first day we decided to go to Pinkworthy Pond (pronounced Pinkery), which was created by damming the headwaters of the River Barle. About halfway there we parked the car and took a path on the right leading to the pond. It was quite large and the water looked blue on this beautiful day – a reflection from the sky. There wasn't another soul in sight and we stood for some time soaking up the atmosphere – moors around us, the Chains ahead with the little River Barle running through. The Barle, Exe and West Lyn rise on Chains Barrow. We started to walk across the Chains but the ground became so boggy that we retraced our steps to the road and drove on to the village of Parracombe, in the valley of the River Hedden. Here we saw the ancient church of St Petrock and the remains of a motte and bailey from Norman times. It was a most enjoyable afternoon.

Next morning, wearing our wellies, we wandered through our lower fields with Thomas and came to a little ditch, filled with water from the recent heavy rain.

Thomas put a paw in, didn't like it, so I quickly scooped him up and deposited him the other side. We were delighted to notice a number of tadpoles swimming in the water and hoped to see some frogs later on. Unfortunately, when we returned a few days later, the water had seeped away due to the warm weather, and I fear the frogs never emerged. I was very disappointed but John assured me that we always had plenty in a more permanent ditch below the house and I had never known this!

We were already getting many enquiries about South Hill, although we hadn't spoken to the estate agents yet. One person was very keen to buy and already had his house up for sale. We didn't mind waiting as we were enjoying our leisure time. Although we put a notice saying 'No Camping' on our top gate, people still turned up and all got sent on to Batsom.

As the weather remained fine we enjoyed some more trips around Exmoor. We were very fascinated by the Doone country but as we had already visited it from the County Gate approach and had seen Oare church, we decided to drive to Malmsmead. This is a little hamlet on Badgworthy Water and there is a field centre here with a picnic area. It is also a popular place to start a walk through the Doone valley, so we parked the car and set off. It was really beautiful alongside the water and surrounded by hills and trees. Not being holiday time, it was quite isolated on that day. It was difficult to realise that *Lorna Doone*, published in 1869, was simply a novel and not a real story. The author, R D Blackmore, must have loved this area very much indeed – understandable as his father was once rector of Oare church, so he would have had an intimate knowledge of it. It was particularly interesting to us that he was reputed to have written part of the book while staying at the Royal Oak Inn in

Withypool. With the sun shining and many birds singing, we were reluctant to leave this magical place and return to the car. A cup of tea brought us back to reality and we drove home.

Another day we visited Porlock, having driven down the notorious Porlock Hill. A busy, interesting village, sheltered by hills on three sides. The other side led to Porlock Weir, about one and a half miles down the road. The small harbour here was once used for trade, but was now very quiet. There was a footpath leading to Culbone church, said to be the smallest parish church in England. We didn't take it, as the church would probably have been shut. There is no public road leading to the tiny hamlet of Culbone.

We returned home across the moors towards Exford, driving through the little village of Stoke Pero. We stopped here to look at the small church, which is one of the highest on Exmoor. Unfortunately its date and dedication are missing but it appeared to be very old.

We were still working mornings to get South Hill ready for selling, so felt we deserved the afternoons off, but time was passing too quickly for us. John painted back-house and the larder to freshen them up. We fetched more gravel from the little beach by the river to fill up potholes in the lane. We both painted our top entrance gate in grey hammerite – anti-rust paint. A great improvement on a rusty white gate.

William Mayo came to sort out some items for Barnstaple Salerooms, mostly belonging to Ted, plus a few we would not require in a new home. He stayed for about one and a half hours, chatting over cups of tea.

We took our remaining seven hens along to Raymond, as we needed to clean out the fowl house. What a job that was! I helped John for about an hour, by which time I was so badly bitten by fleas I was ordered to clear off! Fleas, mosquitoes, horseflies, all loved me but chose to ignore John. It was most unfair.

One day in April George Burnell and a friend came to South Hill with guns and dogs, looking for foxes as Bungy had been losing lambs at Kings. They found no signs, although Bungy still had ewes in our fields, but no lambs yet.

Our regular campers were still asking if we would reconsider opening the camping field but we had to disappoint them. We knew it was unlikely that any buyers would be interested in taking this on. Should anyone want to they would have no difficulty in starting again.

We were still busy with bonfires and sawing up wood for the Rayburn. We had one day of calamities.

Firstly, the electricity was off for the whole day because of work being carried out nearby.

Secondly, when John was backing the tractor to fix to the generator he smashed its rear window. Plenty of glass to clear up!

Thirdly, John discovered the petrol tank on the car was leaking so we were unable to take the furniture to the auction rooms as planned. Fortunately the tank was replaced at Winsford garage the same afternoon, so we were in time for the auction that week.

Chapter Twelve

May started off with hot, sunny weather. Charles and Diana called in to see us. They were keen to buy South Hill and were considering a syndicate with members of their family, but found the asking price too high – as did others from the village who came to look around. Our first keen would-be buyer was having no luck selling his house.

We decided it was time to let Gribble, Booth & Taylor, the estate agents, take over. They suggested an auction date for 20th July, unless it sold before. We hoped it would, as Maggie was already finding us suitable properties in Nailsea!

We had four people interested within a few days, all making various offers between £235,000 and £302,000. The latter offer was from a youngish couple who were living in a lovely property the other side of South Molton. They actually had two houses, one being used as a holiday let. Also land, stabling and a manège course for horses. Despite this they badly wanted to move to Exmoor and they fell in love with South Hill straight away. They immediately put their place on the market, contacted their solicitor and started proceedings. It all looked very promising until two weeks later when they had not received a single enquiry. Peter, the husband, was so anxious that we might sell to somebody else that he put a very large advertisement in a prominent position of a London newspaper. We saw a copy of this and felt sure there would be interest this time.

In the meantime, Maggie had informed us of two suitable properties in Nailsea – a bungalow and a house, each detached with four bedrooms and a quarter of an acre gardens. Just what we wanted, so off we went to view them. The next day we decided on the bungalow, only to be told it had just sold that morning! We couldn't lose the house as well, so I rang to make an offer on that which was later accepted.

Peter rang again to say they had no buyer yet despite their London advert. We now had another couple with two young daughters who also wanted South Hill very badly. They were intending to buy a shop in South Molton and wanted a house with some land to live in, preferably on Exmoor. Mrs W walked through Hayes Wood with me on a glorious afternoon and was very excited. 'It's just what we are looking for,' she exclaimed. 'It will be perfect for the girls.'

They owned a business and house in London and had to sell these first. She admitted they had been on the market for some time. Oh dear! This meant we now had three people all ready to buy but who couldn't sell their own properties. We discovered that the market was very weak at this time, with the exception of cheaper houses.

During all this house anxiety we had bought a new car. Well, not entirely new. It was a Sierra Estate, six months old with 5,000 miles on the clock, and we were very happy with it.

Meanwhile we were getting mixed news from our family. Cathy had passed her driving test at the first attempt and the very next day was in hospital to have her appendix out! Mike rang one evening to say he had a new, and better, job. The very next day he had the radio pinched from his car. The dashboard was broken and the window smashed – it cost £60 to replace the window!

We still had Peter asking about South Hill, so worried that we would sell it to someone else. We wanted him to have it, especially as he had raised his original offer, but we knew we had to sell soon as we would have to put a deposit on the Nailsea house.

When the agent phoned to say he had another person coming to look round I was less than enthusiastic about it.

'We don't want anyone else here unless they have sold their property,' I insisted.

'He has nothing to sell,' he assured me.

It rained the afternoon Mr Meeres came. The first rain for two weeks, so we were not optimistic. However, he was so pleasant, seemed interested and promised to let us know very soon. In fact, he came again next day with a good offer and an agreement to purchase our tractor and large implements. This was a great relief to us, but we now had the awkward duty of letting Peter know. I rang him to explain the situation and to say how sorry we were to disappoint him. He sounded so sad but I think he understood, especially as he was still getting no response to his adverts. The same thing applied to the London family but at least we had not become so in-volved with them.

Bungy had kept forty-one hogs at South Hill from 30th December to 23rd May and had then replaced them with ewes, lambs and rams for five weeks. That would be the last time at our farm for him.

We put a large number of miscellaneous farm items in the Mole Valley Farmers' adverts and had an amazing response. The phone never stopped ringing and people were turning up here eager for bargains. Two people rang for the bale trailer, one from Dorset! The calf dehorning crate drew several replies and we posted a drench gun to St Austell in Cornwall! Within two days of the advert appearing, everything had gone.

In the house, I was still trying to empty the freezer in order to sell that. Between packing and all the other requirements for moving I could have done without making strawberry jam and suchlike.

Our dung spreader had had its day, so we rang a scrap metal merchant to collect it. It was waiting for them outside our top gate, but as they were about to load it with their crane, flames went up! They managed to put the flames out but the lorry blocked the road for some time.

Tess had recently found a new home. She had not been very useful as a farm dog and disappeared frequently, which was particularly difficult at this busy time. Even Thomas was suffering from the turmoil, often off his food and very aware of something unusual going on. We would be taking the three cats to Nailsea with us, but Tess didn't get on too well with them so we were pleased to have her settled in a loving home.

We had a skip delivered for the remainder of our rubbish, which seemed to be never ending. Despite all this we still managed to visit Ted, who seemed reasonably happy in the home. The charge for being there was £205 weekly.

In mid-June we were being asked for the deposit on our Nailsea house, so arranged an overdraft from the bank. On arriving home we found a cheque from Mr Meeres for the items he was purchasing from us, which meant we were able to cancel the overdraft. We were very grateful to him for that.

Now his solicitor wanted to walk around the boundaries of South Hill and to check on the water supply. Although we were getting rain again now it was said to be the driest spring for 200 years! It was decided that someone who understood water should come to inspect it. Fortunately the expert said there was no shortage of water at South Hill and a borehole would produce plenty, which was a great relief.

We arranged 4th July as a provisional date for moving, with Yeates of Clevedon. We were well ahead now with our final clearing out. The freezer was advertised and we had three replies. It was too large for the first two people but luckily it was just what the third person wanted. John took the tractor for service so that it was in good order for Mr Meeres. He removed soot from the Rayburn. We filled the skip in readiness for collection. Beryl came for a last visit and stayed for tea and supper. Days were rushing by, much of the time spent on phone calls to solicitors of both properties.

We attended our last evening service at Exford church and said goodbye to John Atkin. There were so many people we were going to miss, as well as the lovely places around here, but we were sure we had made the right decision.

Thomas was still causing us anxiety. He looked so miserable sitting on the windowsill in the rain, or leaving his food, or disappearing for hours. The other two cats seemed unaware of all the turmoil taking place but Thomas was really upset. Perhaps he was remembering the time when his original owners packed up and moved, leaving him behind.

It was a pleasant and unexpected surprise, on returning from Dulverton one day, to find a card and chocolates from Lydia, Percy and Cedar.

We had our last bonfire. The wardrobe in my bedroom was full of woodworm, so John and Iain took it to pieces and burnt it. They also lopped some trees at the top of the drive to make it easier for the removal van. When Iain and Maggie left they took our lawnmower, clothes and other items home in their motor van.

It was becoming obvious that we would not be moving on the 4th, with no contracts signed yet. I rang Yeates and was told they could manage it on the 11th. I suggested that John Griffin came on the 3rd to arrange the removal and bring us some packing cases.

We had signed the contract for Nailsea at last but were still waiting for the South Hill one. Our solicitor sounded very poorly when I rang him and his assistant was at home feeling ill. Mr Meeres was due to come on the 6th, but due to family illness, this was rearranged for the 10th, just one day before we were hoping to move, and still no contract signed! Actually the Nailsea move was causing concern, regarding the signing of the conveyance. The Nailsea solicitor was unavailable – not surprising as we discovered on the 10th that he was in hospital!

Barry Meeres turned up that evening, by which time John and I were getting frantic with worry. We were packed ready for moving and still no contract.

'Don't worry, my dear, it will definitely be signed for you to go tomorrow,' Mr Meeres assured me. With these positive words and his hand placed sympathetically on my shoulder, I felt we should go ahead with the removal and hope for the best. We didn't sleep well that night!

Next morning dawned fine and sunny, surely a good omen. The removers turned up early and we were ready for them. They worked quickly and very well and finally trundled off up the lane. Now it was time for us to follow. We had our three cats shut safely in an outhouse to stop them wandering off and we were about to get them into carriers ready for the journey when the phone rang. It was Alan, our solicitor, sounding very anxious. 'We still haven't received the contract and cheque from Mr Meeres,' he said. 'Don't move until you hear from me.'

I dared not tell him the removal van was already on its way to Nailsea and in another ten minutes we should have left here also. We had to stay near the phone. As all the chairs had gone we sat on the stairs and waited. It seemed a long, anxious wait but eventually the bell rang. Alan again. 'It's all right now. The signed contract and completion have been faxed through from Coutts' Bank and on to your Nailsea bank. When you get there you will be able to pick up the keys from the estate agent, who is being informed.'

What a relief! Now we could get the cats in their cages. Thomas managed to escape from his but we caught him and secured him well the second time. Then we were away up the lane. Everything looked so beautiful on that sunny summer morning. Memories came flooding back: the first time we had driven down some thirty years before; the frequent happy visits to Uncle Ken and Aunt Dolly over the years: finally, coming here to live with Uncle just four years ago.

We drove across the moor, which was just coming in to brilliant colour, and realised we would never be living in such a beautiful area again. We would miss the little River Barle, our bluebell wood, the moors and the friends we had made. Instead, we would be near our family, the shops, the library, and the doctor – everything suitable for our advancing years!

Above all we would have our happy memories of glorious Exmoor.

Epilogue

Back to Nailsea again. It was just a village when we had left it nineteen years earlier but was now a busy little town. We were lost! Everything had changed and the people we encountered were strangers.

We were frequently asked the way to a certain road which we had never heard of and when John was in the front garden in Station Road cars often drew up with drivers needing directions. John finally kept a street map of Nailsea in our car and they were able to pore over it together!

The following year we bought a motorvan and started our travels – our first holidays for over twenty years. We first went to John O'Groats, Scotland, stopping at Gretna Green and Glasgow on the way up and at Aviemore and Bridge of Allan on the way home.

We visited Edinburgh on a separate occasion, which was a complete washout, as it never stopped raining. We had just bought an umbrella – the type that doesn't blow inside out – but for some reason we couldn't put the wretched thing up! We spent the afternoon dashing from shop to shop, getting very wet and glad to get back to the car.

We decided to pass on the motorvan to Maggie and Iain and were now using the car and booking cottages with self-catering. This gave us complete freedom to go where and when we wanted. We chose the beautiful Yorkshire Dales, a great county; Northumberland with wonderful Holy Island, which can be reached only when the tide is out; Staffordshire with the potteries; Cornwall with its lovely beaches; the Norfolk Broads with its windmills and waterways; the Lake District; Exmouth in Devon, a special favourite; North Wales, with a train trip to the top of Snowdon, and many other places. We never chose to go abroad with such delights available in our own country.

Each year we stayed with David in Chittlehamholt, meeting old neighbours. From here we visited Withypool, to breathe in the pure Exmoor air which we missed so much.

We lost our three cats during the first five years, Christopher in a car accident and Jack and the amazing Thomas through illness. We were very miserable without a cat and through Karen, who later started her own registered charity – 'Bristol's League for Cats' – we started fostering them. This was a very worthwhile venture which I wrote about in a short book, *Cats Tails*. These were all rescue cats or kittens, sometimes feral, which we looked after, or tamed, until we could find kind homes for them.

The fostering finished abruptly when John became ill. In agonising pain one day, he was rushed to hospital and operated on for a strangulated hernia. During the next two years he had open heart and bowel operations and then discovered he had another hernia plus prostate cancer! Three-monthly implants are keeping the latter in check.

We had to move from our large house and garden to an easily managed bungalow with a very small garden. No more holidays or cats. However, we have good friends here, some we have met through attending Christ Church in Nailsea, and I have found time to write three books! These were at the request of our family so that the younger members could enjoy reading of our adventures. Our great granddaughter, aged six and a half, is already reading well and her brother is not far behind. Maybe even a further generation will be interested one day?